Praise for

Grace Meets Grit

and Daina Middleton

"*Grace Meets Grit* is a spot-on guidebook for how women can embrace their individual talents and become indispensable for their organizations. Women at all levels—and the companies for which they work—should take her message to heart; if they do, explosively good results will follow as they'll create more diverse, more innovative, more kind, and more creative teams!"

—Marc Landsberg, founder, CEO SOCIALDEVIANT

"With over 50 percent of today's undergraduate degrees awarded to females, and increasingly more women entering the workforce, it is virtually impossible to lead in any field without managing gender-mixed teams. From the wisdom she has gained through a stellar marketing career, Daina teaches us how to recognize and deliberately employ gender-based attributes of both men and women to transform our organizations through leadership. *Grace Meets Grit* is a must-read for current or aspiring leaders in any industry who are serious about upping their game and effectively leading in today's talent marketplace."

—Monica Pool Knox, head of global talent management, Microsoft

"I cannot speak more highly of Daina and her insights into today's leadership challenges. As a great team leader herself, she has experienced firsthand the significant differences that men and women go through on their leadership journeys. Coaching, training, and encouraging others, Daina helps women grapple with toxic leadership environments, come to terms with their own insecurities, and understand their opportunity to rise up and contribute with grace and brains to the workplace. *Grace Meets Grit* is a phenomenal exploration of important leadership skills."

—Frederique Covington Corbett, SVP/CMO, Visa, Asia Pacific

"Having worked extensively in leadership development for twenty years, never before have I read a more important book about gender communications and leadership. Middleton's evidence-based examination of seven valued leadership behaviors empowers women to harness their natural leadership abilities with confidence. Understanding the combined value of Grace and Grit will allow you to achieve superior results at work and in life. This is a must-read for aspiring female—and male—leaders."

—Amanda Broadnax, leadership and development manager

"Working in diversity and inclusion, I often see women leaders who attain strategic leadership roles but then feel they must adapt their behavior to match that of their male colleagues. In *Grace Meets Grit*, Daina Middleton demonstrates how we can use our authentic and traditional feminine strengths to benefit our teams, and how to dial up our "grit" when the situation calls for it. A must-read for all professional women!

—Lesley Slaton Brown, chief diversity officer, HP Inc.

"We are each born with powerful natural advantages. Yet we must learn how to identify and amplify these advantages, so our work can make a real difference. In this remarkable book, Daina Middleton offers women a new frame to heighten their own unique value and strengths as leaders, to stand out, be heard, and make a real difference in the world. An extraordinary, empowering book from a highly accomplished woman!"

—Sally Hogshead, *New York Times* best-selling author
and creator of the Fascinate System

Grace

— *meets* —

GRIT

Grace
— *meets* —
GRIT

HOW TO BRING OUT THE REMARKABLE, COURAGEOUS LEADER WITHIN

DAINA MIDDLETON

bibliomotion inc.

First published by Bibliomotion, Inc.
39 Harvard Street
Brookline, MA 02445
Tel: 617-934-2427

www.bibliomotion.com

Printed in the United States of America

Print ISBN 978-1-62956-139-4
E-book ISBN 978-1-62956-140-0
Enhanced E-book ISBN 978-1-62956-141-7

I am amazingly fortunate to have a number of remarkable family members who embody Grace and Grit. Some of them have passed and some are just beginning. All of them have had an impact on my life. This book is dedicated to my great-grandmother Nona; grandmothers Tess and Myrtle; my mom, Sandy; my daughter, Mesa; and my granddaughters, Blair and Adelaide.

Contents

Introduction

My first real job in life was fighting rangeland fires for the Bureau of Land Management (BLM) during the summer months of my college years. The work was physically and mentally demanding, dirty, and required hours or days spent in close proximity with coworkers in a very tight space—mostly inside a fire truck. The West is vast and distances can be huge between fires. Experiences on the fire line were intense, and there was no shortage of heart-racing, hazardous, and sometimes life-threatening situations. I was eighteen years old, and this was my first opportunity to observe men and women working together in truly pressure-cooker situations.

The BLM is the agency within the U.S. Department of the Interior that administers more than 247 million acres of public lands in the United States. Most of these acres are in vast sagebrush land tracks in the twelve Western states subject to dry conditions and therefore susceptible to fire.

BLM crews are assigned at the beginning of each summer to a mobile-attack fire engine designed for conquering fast-moving blazes in the wide-open sagebrush country. It's a demanding job, but one that paid well, especially during big fire seasons.

Each summer, I was assigned to one of the larger fire engines that held eight hundred gallons of water. I worked alongside two men. This particular BLM district hired a diverse combination of crews, unusual for the early 1980s. There were all-women crews, all-men crews, and mixed-gender crews. I observed almost immediately that gender combinations affected crew dynamics, within the individual crews as well as between crews.

Mixed-gender crews seemed to be relatively balanced. Moments of misunderstanding definitely occurred—sometimes we had a tendency to want to choose different paths, and how we chose to work was different. My male partners often preferred to work alone. I initially perceived this as a form of martyrdom but eventually learned there was an unwritten hierarchy associated with the various jobs—driving the truck, manning the hose lines, etc. There was no instruction manual that said driving the truck was the top-level job and went to the most senior truck leader; this was just understood. It took me years to earn the right to drive that truck.

Our crew was not as competitive with each other or with other crews as some of the crews with only men, who were more aggressive and also, at times, impulse-driven. The all-male crews were always the first to charge out, taking the fire head-on at top speed, without considering other factors.

On the other hand, women in all-women crews sometimes faced relationship drama, within their own crew and with other crews, though they also could be counted on for support and worked diligently to collaborate with other crews regardless of the gender makeup. These behaviors persisted even when the crews were not on the fire lines. When crews weren't fighting fires, they performed maintenance on public facilities, such as emptying trash and cleaning up campgrounds, or building and repairing fences. Frequently, crews were allowed to choose the job they wanted if more than one option was available. The all-men crews often had strong opinions about their job preferences, whereas the all-women crews were more flexible and not as passionate about the choices. Keeping everyone happy was more important to the women than arguing over chore assignments.

Fighting fires was a unique opportunity to observe gender dynamics in and among teams working in high-risk situations, where quick decisions were often required and the stakes around those decisions meant life or death. I sometimes long for the clarity and efficacy that an emergency situation can bring to work. Trial by actual fire can accelerate the synchronization of crew communication skills more rapidly than anyone can imagine. Each day a number of decisions were made swiftly and acted on, and learning was applied for next time. We became skilled at working through our challenges quickly and adapting on the fly, not wasting time on our differences in communication style and approach, probably because we were more focused on the outcome of the moment.

At the time, I had no awareness of gender differences in leadership behaviors or styles. I did not have enough life or work experience to understand the implications of either. However, this foundational experience of seeing how women and men work, collaborate, and communicate within teams heightened my awareness of diversity nuances in the workplace and inspired me to further explore gender differences in leadership behaviors.

Gender and Leadership Behaviors

As a young woman entering the workforce, I did not fully grasp that men and women inherently communicate differently. Women use communication as a tool to enhance social connections and create relationships. Their leadership style is an extension of this communications style. They care deeply about other individuals and believe relationships are critical to their personal and professional success.

Men, on the other hand, also activate their leadership approach as an extension of their communications style by using communication to achieve tangible outcomes, preserve hierarchy, and avoid failure. Accordingly, men often prefer to work independently, involving others only when they must. The primary means of establishing rank is to instruct others, and prioritizing actions that drive immediate impact is of utmost importance.

When I first entered the ranks of management, I tried to apply the leadership behaviors and communication style that had brought me success in the past. I was disheartened to find that there seemed to be an unwritten set of rules that my male counterparts innately grasped, while I floundered. Years later, I came to recognize that I was not alone in this experience. Many women related similar stories: the established norms of communication and leadership style in their companies were dominantly male, and the talents these women brought to the table were undervalued or did not seem to fit within established structures.

Power from Combining Leadership Styles

As a CEO, I came to realize that the driving forces behind both male and female leadership styles were more powerful when combined—the "get it done now" attitude with a people-inclusive leadership approach was powerful and enabled me to lead my team more effectively. Having both attributes was important within one person, and among those on a team. Thus, Grace meets Grit was born.

This book is divided into two sections. In part 1, we explore the differences between male and female leadership behaviors, derived from innate communication styles, and define "Grace" and "Grit." We examine three different styles of leadership: transactional, transformational, and laissez-faire, and learn how women naturally apply transformational behaviors and why leadership experts view this method as the way of the future.

In part 2, we explore six specific behaviors that are critical to leadership success. We take each one individually, through case studies and research, to understand how Grace and Grit operate differently in the workplace and why having both is a benefit to individuals, teams, and organizations. We also look at why many women struggle to embrace behaviors that express power and confidence. These behaviors are core tenants of leadership success, and women must learn how to overcome the ambivalence sometimes associated with them to embrace confidence and power.

Helping individuals, leaders, teams, and organizations to embrace the strengths within their unique differences is the goal of *Grace Meets Grit*.

Let's get started.

PART I

Gender Differences in Leadership Style

I have been asked during an interview to describe my leadership style. I honestly cannot recall how I responded and I certainly did not respond with "I'm a transformational leader." Nor did I consider the implications of gender on leadership styles until later in my career.

I'm willing to bet that the interviewers did not expect these responses either. Individuals obviously have different leadership styles that are influenced by a number of factors ranging from their age, class, race, cultural and ethnic background, and gender. As we work to diversity organizations, understanding these differences, along with specific leadership styles and behaviors are becoming increasingly important.

Now is the time for us to talk about our different leadership behaviors to facilitate greater understanding and also to consider what organizations are missing by not having these differences within their executive teams.

CHAPTER 1

Understanding Leadership Through Grace and Grit

Kate, a newly minted manager, was excited to attend her very first leadership staff meeting. She had recently been promoted to lead a team of five sales professionals. She had worked hard for this promotion: six years at the company, where she often spent nights and weekends demonstrating to the management team that she had the skills and commitment to move up the chain of command. Kate was simultaneously proud and apprehensive to be the only woman seated at the leadership table and one of the few women represented in senior leadership overall at the company. She felt honored to be pioneering the path for other women in the organization and hoped that company executives would recognize the value of having more women in management.

Kate and her peers, all of them men, were settled into their seats in the conference room when her new boss, John, came in the room a few minutes late and sat down. He appeared on edge and stressed, but, because this was her first meeting, she wasn't sure if he was truly anxious or if he always appeared tense during staff meetings. She watched as he took a deep breath and explained: "We have a situation that I have just been made aware of, so, instead of focusing on the agenda we had planned, we have something more urgent to discuss," he said. "I just learned that we are likely not going to make our revenue numbers this quarter, and we need to change that. This is going to require everyone's immediate and undivided attention for at least the next few weeks."

Missing the revenue quota was not the message the company wanted to send to the marketplace. Leadership had decided to tap everyone in the organization in an effort to generate immediate revenue and reverse the negative outcome for the quarter. The emergency project had been given a name to be a rallying cry for all involved: Code Red.

"We will meet again in the morning, and I want each of you to bring your plan to close the gap," John said. He answered a few questions briefly and then concluded the meeting early so his team could get started on the priority project.

Kate walked out of the room and went directly to her assistant to clear her schedule so that she could focus on Code Red. Then she worked with her assistant to rebook her calendar with a number of new meetings. Kate decided to meet with her entire team so that she could thoroughly explain the situation to them personally. She then requested individual meetings with key members of her staff, a number of her peers, and others in the organization whom she felt could provide good insight into the project. She wanted to ensure that she was prepared to represent their point of view to leaders at tomorrow's meeting.

Her plan was to gather as much information as possible in the organization so that she could walk into the meeting the following morning prepared to make a good first impression in her new role. She asked a number of questions in her encounters with individuals, including inquiring about how they would solve the problem. Her interviews continued late into the night as she gathered perspectives from peers and individuals around the world and assimilated the information in a comprehensive document that she could present the next morning.

She went to bed that night feeling optimistic about the number of individuals she had been able to connect with in a short amount of time and the depth of information they had provided. She thought she had even uncovered a unique understanding about seasonal patterns that had not been considered previously by the team. This discovery had the potential to prevent a Code Red from happening in the future.

What Kate didn't realize is that her male peers took a very different approach to solving Code Red. Rick, also a new manager who was promoted just a month before Kate, left the meeting and also requested that his assistant clear his calendar, so he could focus on Code Red. But this is where the similarity with Kate's behaviors ended. Rick's requested a private conference room where he could focus exclusively and independently on Code Red. He needed a quiet space so he could think without interruption.

Once settled in the room, Rick sent out a number of directive e-mails to his team and peers telling them to perform specific, immediate actions. He instructed each individual to provide him with a status update by the end of the day, so he could be sure appropriate events were set in motion. Later in the evening he used these updates to prepare a summary e-mail to his manager, John, thoroughly outlining the progress made on each of the actions he had initiated, in anticipation of the meeting the following morning. John's other direct reports (all men) followed a very similar approach.

Communication Styles and Leadership Behaviors

The seemingly subtle differences in the actions outlined in this example are what this book is all about. Rick, and his male peers, had a specific approach to solving the Code Red problem, one that most leaders in organizations would be familiar with, because, statistically, the majority of leaders are men. This leadership approach is based on the male communication style and is unconsciously the default approach in many companies. Rick and his male peers focused on directive actions that would have immediate impact. The e-mail they sent to John at the end of the day was an important status acknowledgement. Rick wanted John to know that he understood how important this project was, and to assure him that a number of immediate actions were already in motion to solve the problem.

John did not anticipate that his male managers would approach their preparation for the meeting in such a different way than Kate, nor was he specific about his expectations beyond setting the time of the next meeting. John didn't think he needed to be specific, because he had always operated this way and his male managers seemed to intuit his expectations.

Kate's approach was dramatically different, because her leadership approach to solving Code Red was largely based on her female communication style. She prioritized relationships first, ensuring her team understood the problem and heard it directly from her. She arranged time to meet with as many individuals as possible to gather information and ensure every person was well represented in the feedback. Not only did she feel the information others provided was valuable, she felt she had an obligation to represent the ideas of each and every team member up through the management chain of command.

As Kate conducted her interviews, she sought out information that was relevant not only to solving the immediate revenue gap but also to preventing a future Code Red. Finally, while she had assimilated her thoughts and prepared herself for the morning meeting, she didn't consider informing John about her progress and assuring him of her dedication to Code Red as a top priority before the meeting as her male peers did. While relationships and big-picture thinking were at the top of Kate's mind, status and immediate outcomes were the priorities for her male counterparts.

Misunderstandings Arising from Style Differences

This was Kate's first opportunity to make a good impression on the management team. She handled the urgent situation with what she felt were her best tools: personal outreach to each member of her team, listening and gathering information from many sources, producing multiple ideas and solutions, and thinking forward about the future. But did she actually make a good impression on her male boss and peers? Think about the following:

- Did Kate blow it by not sending an e-mail to John, detailing her progress, before the meeting?

- Did Kate feel left out, wondering if she had missed critical expectations in the staff meeting, or perhaps that others had discussed a plan without her?
- Did John recognize the value of the forward-looking material Kate brought that might prevent future Code Red situations?
- Whom did John judge to be more competent at solving Code Red, Kate or Rick, in light of John's leadership expectations' being based on the male communication style of immediate action and status?

Code Red is a real workplace situation that played out just as it is described here, though the names have been changed. The actions of female versus male managers in this scenario are a classic case of differences in gender communication and leadership style. When we do not recognize or acknowledge that men and women tend to have different leadership strengths, these gender style differences often create minor misunderstandings. Sometimes, as in Kate's case, these differences can leave women leaders wondering if they missed a set of instructions or feeling less competent than their male counterparts. At worst, I have seen situations where women lose their jobs because a male manager didn't understand their different, yet valid, leadership style.

While you may not have experienced a Code Red, you likely have experienced work situations where your own communication and leadership style differed from that of your peers. I have witnessed situations like this many times throughout my career, but it took me years to recognize the source behind these behavior differences.

Differing Communication Objectives

One reason why women's communications style differs from men's is that the two genders have differing objectives. A woman's leadership style is an extension of her communications style. Women use communication as a tool to enhance social connections and create relationships. They tend to care deeply about other individuals and believe relationships are critical to their personal and professional success. My own research has found that women believe they have an obligation as a leader to ensure that the opinions of others are voiced. When solving a problem, women often focus on the bigger picture and longer-term solution, even if it means sacrificing immediate activities or disrupting a tight timeline.

Men also activate their leadership approach as an extension of their communications style by using communication to achieve tangible outcomes, preserve hierarchy, and avoid failure. Accordingly, men often prefer to work independently, involving others only when they must. They are most comfortable relying on their own ideas and solutions, because maintaining independence is vital to their success. In this status-driven setting, the primary means of establishing rank is to instruct others. Prioritizing actions that drive immediate impact is of utmost importance to men.

Subtle Leadership Differences

The idea that men and women approach leadership from different priorities is often overlooked, primarily because the differences in style are often subtle and have not been thoroughly explored or even acknowledged. Or, if they are, it's in a manner that either encourages women to adapt to the male standard, or the issue is conceded as simply not addressable. The accepted leadership standard is largely built on the male communication style, and companies rarely focus on addressing this disparity as part of the overall issue of gender equality in the workplace.

Inadequacy of the Equality Conversation

Gender in the workplace is not a new topic. Awareness around the need for gender equality today is not lacking. In fact, in some cases, I sense weariness inside organizations that have worked in their own ways to address gender issues. A renewed emphasis on gender in the workplace is also not surprising, given that conversations around gender equality have reignited over the last few years, thanks in part to passionate individuals, such as Sheryl Sandberg, Gloria Steinem, Melissa Gates, Hillary and Chelsea Clinton, and many others. As a result, a number of organizations have created objectives for managing gender bias and implemented training programs on gender bias.

Unfortunately, research has shown that neither gender-bias training nor a heightened awareness about gender equality is having an effect on changing organizational behavior.[1] As a former CEO, I encountered situations where men and women had gender-related communications misunderstandings, especially in the management ranks. As my awareness grew, I began to recognize these challenges were happening in other organizations as well, and I initiated conversations within my own team and with other leaders to heighten awareness and seek solutions.

Through the lens of heightened awareness, I observed situations in which misinterpretations caused disruptions in the workplace and, in two cases where I could not influence the outcome, cost women their jobs. I began to wonder if this wasn't a contributing factor to women dropping out of the leadership pipeline altogether. To ameliorate the situation, I began experimenting with workshops and coaching sessions that I specifically created to drive awareness around gender differences and drive behavior change in the workplace.

Change Driven by Understanding Gender Differences

Helping men, women, and organizations uncover a different and deeper conversation about gender communication styles in the context of leadership behaviors is incredibly rewarding. For women, it is about helping them understand that they are not imagining things or suddenly going crazy, and that the rules do appear to actually change when women are at the management level. This is driven by the fact that the male leadership style is largely still the corporate standard, because—let's face it—men are still in charge. Consequently, there really is a secret code in the mostly male leadership ranks. Even though it isn't designed to exclude women in most cases, it simply doesn't *include* them either, because of the gap in understanding the differences in the communication approach between the genders.

Advantages of the "Grace Meets Grit" Approach

A few years ago, I stumbled upon a new way to think about and address the particular strengths that men and women each bring to the leadership table. I was leading a group exercise comprising ten men and ten women working in pairs. I came up with the idea to use the word "Grace" to describe the more female approach to communication and leadership style, and "Grit" to describe the more male approach. It was simple, and fun, and became a breakthrough concept for the group, and for me, that changed my approach to gender training thereafter.

Somehow, by using words that oversimplified and typecast the behaviors, individuals could open up and talk more freely about differences in a way that wasn't perceived to be offensive. The tension that sometimes exists when individuals described how "women do this" or "men do that" simply disappeared. Grace and Grit were also easy to remember and became a touchstone to remind people about the workshop. Occasionally my own team will remind me, jokingly, by asking, "Did you leave Grace at home today?"

After having a clearer understanding about the differences between Grace and Grit, men and women both acknowledged that neither was right or wrong. Rather, Grace and Grit are better together—both within an individual who has elements of both approaches, and within an organization, where women and men who excel personally at Grace and Grit add value to the whole. In my workshops, I often get to witness Grace truly meeting Grit for the first time and vice versa, through attendees gaining a better understanding of the strengths that each brings to the workplace and a clearer perspective of how to work together more effectively. Grace meets Grit can help teams recognize and apply the strengths of individuals through the lens of their differences. Looking back to the Kate scenario, things might have unfolded differently if the team had understood the traits of Grace and Grit and how they complement each other:

- John would have clearly outlined his expectations to every member of his team in the initial meeting, including his expectation about the update e-mail.

- Kate would have understood that she was expected to acknowledge the urgency of the situation and communicate her immediate actions to John without being instructed to do so.
- At the same time, Kate should have continued to prioritize staying close to her team, gathering a broad swath of information from others, and seeking solutions to prevent a Code Red from happening in the future.
- Rick and his peers would have been as proactive about communicating with their own team as they were about initiating immediate actions.
- John would have understood that Rick and his peers would likely focus more on immediate actions, but he might remind them to involve their teams.
- Finally, John would have asked Kate to gather ideas from every part of the organization and explore solutions to prevent it from happening in the future.

When Grace meets Grit, organizations leverage the assets of both men and women in the ranks of leadership. Individuals begin to understand that each person brings innate styles that are valuable, and organizations are empowered to tap these unique and desirable skills. Men and women begin to recognize hidden nuances in their communication and leadership styles that have never been discussed, let alone understood. These new insights have the power to change behavior in a way that gender-bias training alone cannot provide. In the next chapter, we explore more deeply how the concepts of Grace and Grit play out in today's workplace.

CHAPTER 2

Why Grace Needs Grit

According to a 2009 study conducted by Zenger Folkman, women employees make up 53 percent of the workforce population when they enter the workplace as individual contributors. By the time they become supervisors, women represent only 37 percent of the population. With each rise in level within an organization, the population of women continues to shrink. Women compose 30 percent of the mid-manager roles, 26 percent of the vice presidents, 14 percent of senior executives, and just 3 percent of CEOs.[1]

Despite the fact that women outnumber men when they first enter the workplace, far fewer women advance to become senior managers. The disheartening statistics reveal a discouraging story: Only 3 percent of CEOs in Fortune 500 companies are women, and a recent study indicates these numbers are declining, not increasing. The newest survey from the S&P Capital IQ research and analysis company found that only twenty-one women held the top job among S&P 500 companies. This is down from twenty-five in 2014. Women CEOs lag men CEOs in terms of tenure by two years,[2] and a mere 8 percent of executive positions are held by women.[3] The percentage of women holding board positions is also meager.

The need to find a solution is acute. In large organizations, women are dropping out of the management ranks at an alarming rate. While the statistics vary slightly around the world, this pattern is consistent globally, and it's not a pretty picture. According to a study by LeanIn .org and McKinsey & Company, *Women in the Workplace*, women face greater barriers to advancement and a steeper path to senior leadership than their male counterparts. The momentum is not headed in the right direction. In fact, at the rate of current progression for women in the leadership pipeline, it would take more than a hundred years for the upper reaches of the corporate world to achieve gender parity.[4]

Management's Unique Challenges for Women Leaders

Why do women continue to drop out despite the rising awareness around gender equality and bias? The answer is complex and has cultural, organizational, and personal implications. Women in business often experience disillusion, isolation, loneliness, and discouragement as they rise in the leadership ranks. The challenge is particularly critical when women take that first step into a leadership position.

It was that way for me. Through the years, I found that I was not alone in having these feelings. Time after time, I heard women who had just made the transition to management say they had felt similar doubts about their abilities, their career path, and their decision to join the ranks of management. They talked about confronting a "secret code" and being torn about whether to keep focusing on the skills and abilities that had made them successful before joining the management ranks or adapting to the organizational standard. That standard, they said, often felt foreign and not necessarily best for the organization as a whole. Creating a conversation different from the one happening about equality became the driving force behind my writing this book.

My own doubts about leadership and management began the year I was first promoted to managing a team. It also was the year that I felt miserable in my job for the first and only time in my career. My feelings of inadequacy and isolation were overwhelming at times. I was torn, because I sensed my team appreciated my leadership approach and I knew I was providing them with good support and guidance, while, at the same time, something still didn't feel right. My manager, who was a man, kept telling me how thankful I should feel to have the leadership position.

Navigating the Secret Management Code

At first, I was elated about reaching this significant milestone in my career, pleased that I was taking what I knew to be a vital step toward continuing advancement. Up to this point, I had been successful by demonstrating that I could effectively work with all levels of the organization. But, in this new position, it was as if the rules of the game had suddenly changed and I no longer knew what they were. No one ever informed me about these rules, nor, as I said, did anyone seem to have a manual. In fact, no one talked about it at all.

Instead, I would find myself attempting to solve problems in the same manner as I had before my promotion, only to find my methods seemed no longer to be effective. Though I sensed there was a problem, I couldn't quite put my finger on it, but from the reactions of my male peers and male boss, I knew my assessment to be accurate. My boss was actually supportive in having the conversation, but he could not really diagnose the problem either. It boiled down to the fact that I missed deliverables that everyone else seemed to know about and I didn't, or I focused on the wrong things. But these were subtle mistakes, and though my boss was not exactly happy with me, he took no punitive action.

I fumbled around, using trial and error in an attempt to find my way. Doubt set in, followed by frustration and despair. The disparaging voice in my head became active: Maybe the job or task was too challenging. Maybe I was not ready for management or leadership. Maybe I was unworthy and had made a mistake. I began to doubt the decision to leave my previous role, which had been highly successful and which I knew and loved, and longed to go back to it.

I never spoke to anyone about these feelings of inadequacy and frustration. I was ashamed that I needed help. I assumed it was something that I had to deal with myself or forfeit my leadership position. It never occurred to me that I was not alone, or the only one to feel this way. I only learned later that many other women had experienced similar feelings after joining the management ranks.

Promotion to Management Shines a Light on Differences

The transition from individual contributor to manager is the moment where Grace meets Grit for the first time. Transitioning to a supervisory role marks a time when, statistically, women are more likely to have peers and a boss who are men. This is often when, for the first time, a woman recognizes just how different her approach to leadership is compared with the male standard, even though she might not understand this is causing her dissatisfaction.

Confronting the Male Leadership Standard

Women are most likely to encounter the male leadership standard when they become managers. The result often is that, as a woman rises through the ranks, surrounded by men and reporting to a man, she suddenly recognizes that she does not fit in with the standard mold for how leaders should behave. Companies are accustomed to leadership behaviors of successful executives to be associated with men.[5] It is the unspoken cultural norm.

As a consequence, women leaders are expected to adapt to the leadership expectations of their male counterparts and bosses. When they don't and they receive negative feedback for it, female leaders may try to adjust their behaviors to fit the expectation. This adjustment might not be what you would expect. Some women try to change their style to be much more Grit, hoping to fit in with the guys. Other women try to stick with the cultural norms associated more with women leaders, emphasizing Grace. And worst, some may swing wildly between both, depending on the situation. Regardless, the impact on a woman's career is likely to be negative.

Encountering Cultural and Behavioral Expectations

There are both descriptive and prescriptive gender stereotypes regarding how women should behave in organizational settings. These are based on a blend of cultural, behavioral, and organizational norms. These norms are often subtle, yet critical. Finding the right balance of leadership behaviors while avoiding stereotypes can be challenging and may have a draining effect for women who find themselves in an environment where their leadership behaviors do not align with the expectations and behaviors shared by the organization.

Caliper Corporation, a talent management company, conducted a study in 2014 that found when women leaders adopted a more masculine style in an attempt to adapt to the stereotype threat, their direct peers rated them as less warm. Peers were also less willing to comply with the request of these women leaders when compared with men leaders who made the same requests.[6] The seeming tradeoff between respect and likeability may cause a woman leader to downplay her femininity or soften a hard-charging style, both of which can be important leadership assets.

The challenge of trying to learn the aspects of a new job in management while simultaneously conforming to perplexing and often inconsistent leadership standards is exhausting and can be ultimately self-defeating. The time and energy that must be spent juggling these complexities of a leadership position may explain the feelings of disillusionment and unhappiness described by so many women. It also may explain why women choose not to pursue leadership positions, or drop out of them altogether.

"I thought something was wrong with me and began questioning every decision," said a young woman who described to me her transition about being a first-time manager in the tech industry. "I wondered if the move to management had changed me somehow, because I was not seeing or valuing things the same way as before," she said. "I even questioned my own sanity at one point. I thought I had made a mistake in choosing the [management] role. Maybe I wasn't ready, or good enough."

Like me, and so many others, the feeling of isolation was unnerving, especially when male peers didn't seem to face the same challenges, fit in better, and got it—whatever "it" was.

Women who focus on how others perceive them are less clear about their goals, less open to learning from failures, and less capable of accurately assessing their own performance. Overinvestment in one's image diminishes the emotional and motivational resources available for becoming an inspiring, driven, decisive, confident, powerful, and resilient leader. These behaviors are integral to leadership success and, because of subtle nuances, can be challenging for women to realize. These behaviors are the core focus of *Grace Meets Grit* and described in detail in part 2.

Impacts of Perceptions About Leadership Behavior

The realization that the workplace culture is biased against you, places you at a disadvantage, and jeopardizes your job is devastating and can have a lasting negative impact on self-confidence and performance. Women are three times more likely than men to say they have personally missed out on an assignment, promotion, or raise because of their gender. This perception increases as a woman rises in seniority, with only 28 percent of senior-level women rating themselves as very happy with their careers, compared with 40 percent of senior-level men.[7]

Regardless of gender, people become leaders by developing a sense of purpose and internalizing a leadership identity. Internalizing a sense of oneself as a leader is part of a process of repeated positive reinforcements contributing to feelings of competency. A person asserts leadership by taking purposeful action, such as convening a meeting to discuss an issue that needs to be addressed. Others affirm or resist the action, thus encouraging or discouraging subsequent assertions. According to Hermina Ibarra, Robin Ely, and Deborah Kolb, writing for *Harvard Business Review*, these interactions inform a person's sense of self as a leader on the basis of how others view her fitness for the role.[8]

When we act and others do not support our actions, self-confidence diminishes and we lose the desire to experiment in the future and to seek additional opportunities.[9] Without affirmation, leadership identity is stunted and eventually withers. The result is often a withdrawal from the leadership ranks.

Persistence of the Male Leadership Standard

There is a two-fold problem inherent in the process of leadership affirmation for women as they move into management. First, a male standard of leadership is most often used as the standard by which the effectiveness of the leadership is being judged. The cultural norm of leadership is one based on the leadership qualities associated with men, which I call "Grit." A woman's leadership behaviors may be dismissed or discounted because they may be inconsistent with this style of leadership even though the characteristics may be just as effective, or even more effective. What I call "Grace" leadership characteristics are valued less because they are outside of the norm.

Even in this day and age, many in the corporate world still deem a man to be more qualified to hold a leadership position than a woman. In a recent study by LeanIn.org and McKinsey & Company, 80 percent of respondents believed that both men and women make equally good business leaders, but 43 percent felt businesses are not ready to hire women for top executive positions.[10]

This study also found that men still hold the majority of positions with profit-and-loss responsibilities. Moreover, because these types of positions provide critical preparation for senior roles, leaders holding these positions are on a better track to be promoted. Companies are working to implement mentoring and sponsorship programs directed at women, but there are challenges for this strategy as well.

Research has also shown that men and women experience networking and sponsorship differently. Both are considered vital to success and advancement in the leadership ranks. Women tend to be mentored, while men tend to be sponsored. The difference is important. Mentoring is about giving someone advice. Sponsorship is about championing someone's advancement.

The LeanIn.org and McKinsey study revealed that nearly two-thirds of men received sponsorship support from senior leaders, compared with just over a third of women. Given the fact that men are more likely to hold senior leadership positions already and therefore will be the ones providing the sponsorship support or key network contacts, men clearly have the advantage of receiving the backing required to advance.

Furthermore, this study found that men and women develop segregated networks. Having a strong network to find a champion can be an important succession strategy. Although a man's network is similar in size to that of a woman's, the man's network is predominantly composed of men. If men hold most senior leadership positions and men have more access to these leaders through networking and sponsorships, then women have a disadvantage when attempting to secure a leadership position.

The Inadequacy of Bias-Awareness Training

Organizations understand a gender-gap problem exists, but those attempting to address it through gender-bias programs alone are missing a fundamental insight, one that attention to bias training and gender equality does not address. This insight is that men and women may share the same experiences but do so through completely different perspectives. This often results in men and women thinking and talking past one another. It's almost as if they speak different languages. This makes the problem of increasing the number of women in the ranks of leadership more complicated.

According to Kathy Caprino, author of *Breakthrough: The Professional Guide to Claiming a Life of Passion, Power, and Purpose*, these disparities are grounded in core differences of neurobiology and cultural training.[11]

Alexandra Kalev, at the University of California at Berkeley, and her colleagues examined the effectiveness of approaches that organizations commonly use to promote diversity. She found that efforts to reduce managerial bias through diversity training and diversity evaluations were the least effective methods of increasing the proportion of women in management.[12]

Changing Workplace Behavior Toward Women

What did prove to be successful in changing behavior toward women, Kalev and her colleagues found, were exercises that mimic actual work scenarios and leadership behaviors and that reveal to the participants how women and men perform differently in those situations.[13] By delving deeper into these experiences, men and women were able to develop a greater appreciation for the diverse and subtle underlying differences present in the workplace.

I have used a similar approach in performing organizational workshops, where a common workplace scenario is provided to a group of twenty individuals. Each individual is asked to write down specific actions he or she would take in response to the scenario. The teams in these workshops were then paired into mixed-gender teams of two and were asked to share with their partner what they had written down.

Inevitably, the men described taking steps to set up a separate space where they could focus on the situation, followed by a series of directive actions, such as sending e-mails to team members or instructing others about actions they thought would solve the problem. Women, on the other hand, described a more inclusive approach, such as gathering people together for a special meeting to gain input and consensus, individually and across groups. These exercises were effective at helping participants recognize, understand, and appreciate the differences and value the benefits the diverse perspectives brought to the organization.

Academic research on psychological gender differences has shown that, while women use communication as a tool to enhance social connections and create relationships, men use language to reinforce and maintain status and achieve tangible outcomes. This has huge workplace implications. There are consequences for not taking these differences into account as we do our jobs. As Deborah Tannen, an expert in the role gender plays in the workplace, says in her book *You Just Don't Understand*, "a man and a woman can interpret the same conversation differently, even when there is no apparent misunderstanding."[14]

Equal, Not the Same

In our time, when gender equality is highly advocated, there is a general assumption that men and women think, feel, and behave the same way in most situations. *Equal* literally means *the same*. In reality, because the underlying purpose for the communication is different, rarely do men and women behave the same. This is what causes misunderstanding, confusion, and frustration.

Sally Hogshead, *New York Times* best-selling author of *How the World Sees You*, has been gathering data used to interpret the actions and preferences of an individual through the eyes of others. She used ten years of research to identify individual communication advantages and found that men are two times more likely than women to lead through what she calls a "Power Advantage." The Power Advantage is about leading through status, authority, and influence. In contrast, her research has shown that women leaders are three times more likely to lead through what she calls the "Passion Advantage," or leading through relationships.

Physiological Differences Driving Behavioral Differences

These different communication tendencies are driven by physiological differences in addition to the cultural ones. They are present at work and manifest themselves in everyday interactions. Bias training alone does not address these underlying communication differences in the context of leadership behaviors or everyday work scenarios, and this may explain why bias training does not change employee behaviors.

Beyond the divergence in communication and leadership styles, recent neuroscience discoveries have revealed differences between male and female brains that reinforce behavioral dissimilarities. These discoveries also confirm that gender-based behavior distinctions are not only the result of cultural and environmental conditioning.

Theodore Satterthwaite and his fellow researchers at the University of Pennsylvania found striking differences in neural wiring of men and women that lends credence to the idea of gender-based communication patterns. Men showed greater neural connectivity from front to back and within one hemisphere, suggesting their brains are structured to facilitate connectivity between perception and action. In contrast, in the female brain, wiring goes between the left and right hemispheres, suggesting that women facilitate communication between analytical thinking and intuition.[15] Whether cultural, behavioral, physiological, or biological—or a combination of all—the differences between how men and women communicate are real and have vital workplace implications.

Benefits of Embracing Diversity

Embracing differences in leadership behaviors begins with accepting the fact that men and women think and act differently in the workplace because men and women are fundamentally different. Not stronger or weaker, not better or worse—simply different. Having different leadership styles and approaches to solving workplace situations is a good thing. Diversity brings value to individuals, teams, and organizations alike.

Statistics consistently validate that having women in leadership positions improves company performance. According to a new report by MSCI, the U.S.-based financial index provider, companies with women directors generate a 36 percent higher return on equity.[16] A Credit Suisse analysis of large companies with and without female directors published in 2014 reported that the stock market performance of organizations with women on their boards was 5 percent better than those with only men.[17]

Companies' investment in women leaders pays off, because they stick around longer. Women are loyal leaders, especially at the management level. Compared with men at the same level, women at the level of senior vice president are 20 percent less likely to leave their company, and women in the C-suite (CEO, CIO, etc.) are about half as likely to leave.[18]

Women's Later Peaking in Performance

Furthermore, companies are not taking advantage of key talent when they are in their prime. Writing in *Business Insider*, Bob Sherman, COO of the leadership consultancy Zenger Folkman, cited research from his company that determined that women leaders' effectiveness exceeds that of their male counterparts at age forty and does not peak until age sixty. Why does a woman's leadership effectiveness peak later in life? Beyond the obvious factors that affect younger women, such as having a divided focus earlier in life with family demands, the study attributes the difference to the fact that women consistently practice self-improvement, primarily because they believe they need to perform "twice as well to be thought of as half as good."[19]

Leveraging talent will become increasingly important for organizations in years to come. Data indicates that companies will face talent shortfalls in the future, and solving the gender gap could actually eliminate the talent shortage and grow the global economy. A 2015 study found that, if women were placed in labor market roles, the global annual GDP would increase by as much as $28 trillion by the year 2025.[20] Today, women are half the world's working-age population but generate only 38 percent of GDP.

Benefits of Women's Innate Transformational Leadership

The most compelling case for having women in leadership may be that women more naturally apply what is arguably the leadership style of the future: transformational leadership. Companies are adopting transformational leadership in an effort to meet the increased demands of collaboration in a highly competitive global market and the requirements of a young, demanding workforce.[21] In a time when a company's most valuable asset is harnessing the hearts and minds of employees, effective leadership is a must. Transformational leadership can provide organizations with unique differentiation in attracting and retaining young talent, including those in the millennial generation, and driving organizational performance and is, therefore, a powerful leadership skill. Transformational leaders act as inspirational role models, motivate others to go beyond the confines of their job descriptions, encourage creativity and innovation, foster good human relationships, and develop the skills of their followers. These are the qualities I refer to as "Grace."

Unfortunately, this emphasis on connection, empathy, consensus building, collaboration, and questioning is often misconstrued as the inferior leadership style. During my career, I have witnessed two women lose their jobs because their managers, who were men, did not value or understand their approach to problem solving. Instead of perceiving that these two talented young women leaders followed a different approach to decision making, their bosses judged them to be incapable of solving problems because their process was not the cultural norm.

These women involved many more individuals in the decision process, which meant taking more time. Their solutions addressed the bigger picture—and, proactively, future problems—in addition to the more immediate ones. It was a progressive approach to problem solving that fit the transformational model. Through a better understanding about how communication style is directly tied to leadership style for both genders, women can have greater success in management positions. This is especially true in environments where they are surrounded by male peers and have a man for a boss.

The key insight is that this success does not come because women change their innate approach to leadership or adopt the male standard of leadership to fit in; rather, it is important that they embrace strengths they naturally bring to leadership and hold onto them. Recognizing the differences enables women to better understand the leadership environment that they are entering and level-set expectations about what they face when working closely with a fundamentally different style. Retaining their intrinsic superpower and transformational leadership style actually benefits the entire organization, in addition to improving their personal success in ascending the leadership ladder.

Transformational Leadership and Women

While women more often exhibit the characteristics of transformational leadership naturally, the leadership style is actually androgynous, meaning it incorporates both masculine and feminine behaviors.

This is where Grace meets Grit in the context of leadership behavior. Both women and men can use the transformational leadership style to become remarkable, courageous leaders. This androgynous mixing of the masculine and the feminine, or the style of leadership where Grace meets Grit, will create the next generation of inspiring, driven, decisive, confident, powerful, resilient leaders.

This book focuses on the blending of these leadership behaviors and transformational leadership. Using divisive language, such as "men do this" or "women do that," can cause tensions and trigger biases that impede progress. And we all understand that the definition of gender is broad today. Instead of framing these differences as a battle pitting men against women, I use the term "Grit" to describe how men tend to display leadership behaviors, and "Grace" for the leadership style more associated with women. This is an intentional overgeneralization designed to inspire the conversation.

Neither leadership style is right or wrong. Having a mix of both is best. Through a blend of Grace and Grit, organizational cultures can evolve to accept and actively seek out a wider spectrum of "good" leadership practices. This will create the transformational leadership style of the future and an environment that invites and inspires more women leaders to participate.

That future requires that women see other women in leadership, as role models. Women recognize that promoting more female leaders as role models is a bigger issue than parity—it would result in an improvement in the quality of life for all women within an organization. Unfortunately, fewer than 20 percent of men believe that having more women in top leadership positions would improve women's lives at work.[22] Because men hold the majority of leadership positions and are therefore making most of the leadership decisions for organizations, it is they who must understand what their organization is missing by not having women represented in leadership.

Given our increasingly complex and competitive global economy, organizations have an even greater need to ensure that the most talented employees rise to the top. It is my hope that, through Grace meets Grit, women will bring their real, transparent, honest, and authentic selves to work and be recognized, valued, and appreciated for their unique contributions.

The Competitive Advantage of Collaboration

According to an article in the January/February 2016 issue of *Harvard Business Review*, organizations are becoming increasingly global and cross-functional. Consequently, there is a growing need for more effective teamwork and collaboration. In fact, the magazine's research indicates that the time spent on collaborative activities has increased by more than 50 percent over the past twenty years.[23]

Research conducted by the authors across three hundred organizations found that the distribution of collaborative work within the organization comes from just 3 to 5 percent of the employee population—primarily driven by the fact that certain individuals had a "giving mindset" and a desire to help others, driving overall organizational performance. The research found that desire for these individuals to help others tended to spread within the organization because this help improved the others' own performance and reputation. This demonstrates just how important collaboration is within organizations today.

In fact, an additional study, led by Li Ning of the University of Iowa, indicates that single individuals who contribute beyond the scope of their role to help others can actually drive team performance more than all the other members combined.[24] Most interesting in the *Harvard Business Review* article was that the team found that the majority of these individuals having a "giving mindset" were women. Women were often thought of as more communal and caring in their respective organizations, and as a result were expected to provide mentoring and training to more-junior staff members, recruit new hires, and attend even optional meetings. The unfortunate consequence of this additional burden was that women experienced greater emotional exhaustion and a higher tendency to burn out than their male counterparts.

CHAPTER 3

The Differences Between Grace and Grit

"Charming." I puzzled at the word on the page, even though I had reread it several times. Charming? Charming was not a compliment. Charming was fluffy. How many CEOs are described as charming? Out of all the adjectives my boss could have chosen to describe me, he had chosen the word "charming."

Actually, the words were "charming," "assertive," and "compelling," but I was stuck at "charming." I was not flattered. In my mind, charming seemed to be a gender-biased descriptor, and I was pissed. I doubted he would have described any of his other direct reports, who were all men, as charming. I was a C-suite executive. Why couldn't he have found a more leadership-admired word to describe my effectiveness?

I was CEO of Performics at the time, in 2011. The leadership team of my company annually selected a few promising individuals to participate in leadership development through an executive coaching process. I had chosen to participate in order to lead by example and to quell any rumors that the coaching processes were intended only for those with leadership problems.

I was excited to take part, because I had never before received any executive coaching and considered feedback to be a valuable part of my self-development. I was also particularly eager to hear what my boss thought about my performance, because I hadn't received much in the way of feedback from him. I operated quite independently, which is understandable for a senior leader, but welcomed his suggestions, nonetheless.

The coach had collected responses, using the same set of questions, from my direct reports, peers, and boss. She then brought the completed report to my office so that I could read the responses out loud and we could discuss them. The report had loads of valuable feedback, but "charming" was the only word that stuck with me at the time.

Today, I have a completely different perspective on the word and can fully appreciate the value of Grace in my own leadership style, "charming" included. The executive coaching experience was a gift and a lesson in the process of accepting and embracing my inner Grace, which I define as the emotionally intelligent, people-oriented side of leadership behaviors. Think of Grace as those behaviors focused on relationship-based communication and leadership. For Grace, the entire purpose of communicating, inside and outside of the workplace, is to establish and maintain intimacy.

Grace Behaviors and Motivations

- Grace shares personal details and feelings, complimenting others out of a desire to build and maintain relationships and to build mutual understanding and mutual support.
- Grace respectfully shares speaking time with others, demonstrating respect and maintaining balance in communication and relationships.
- Grace asks questions, rather than using commanding language, as an approach to leading and influencing.
- Grace desires to create an atmosphere of respect and teamwork that intentionally de-emphasizes hierarchical relationships and builds on intrinsic motivation.
- Grace prefers to work with others in an effort to maintain relationships, and reaches out to others when under stress.

On the other hand, we have Grit, which represents the side of leadership behaviors that wants to "get it done" while considering the political ramifications. Think of Grit as representing those behaviors that are focused on immediate outcomes and hierarchical ramifications. For Grit, the entire purpose of communicating, inside and outside of the workplace, is to achieve tangible results and maintain status.

Grit Behaviors and Motivations

- Grit uses directive and commanding language in a desire to communicate efficiently, reinforce hierarchy, and demonstrate responsibility.
- Grit focuses on solutions and actions first, and is sometimes impatient with "small talk" because of a desire to get to tangible outcomes and achieve goals as quickly as possible.
- Grit challenges others' points of view or plays the "devil's advocate," to gather more information or gain a better understanding of the issues.
- Grit prefers to work independently in an effort to maintain status and better control immediate outcomes, especially when under stress.
- Grit will take up space in the room, or in another's space, to establish authority and display confidence and power—all hierarchy signals.

Though I got stuck on "charming," the feedback report contained other words, including "assertive" and "compelling." But he had said something else that described my leadership qualities: "She is a bit strong-willed and speaks her mind. I think people are a bit scared of her. Daina challenges people. She challenges me. She's such a driver."

In fact, on the DiSC (Dominance, Influence, Steadiness, Conscientiousness) assessment, which was also part of my coaching process, these Grit qualities emerged as my most dominant leadership dimension. The instrument assessed me as a high *D*, for dominance. According to William Moulton Marston, who created the DiSC-assessment approach, this means I am a "demanding, forceful, decisive, inquisitive, self-assured, adventuresome risk-taker." As we have already discussed, Grit is the results-focused, status-conscious side of leadership.

Grace showed up in my DiSC assessment as well, through my second-highest dimension, as an *I*, for influential. The adjectives that DiSC uses to describe *I*'s are the same that I would use to describe Grace: "pleasant, sociable, generous, poised, confident, convincing, and [yes] . . . . charming."

I no longer believe that I have to choose between being decisive and charming. I can, and do, choose to apply one or the other, or both on most days. I have learned that having the ability to combine relationship skills with confidence-driven leadership abilities can be beneficial to any workplace situation. I have also come to understand that a leader who is relationship oriented is more likely to use transformational leadership, which is a progressive leadership style.

Engaging Followers Through Transformational Leadership

Transformational leadership is a charismatic approach to leadership that encourages employees to take ownership of company goals, and provides inspirational motivation. It is represented by the word "compelling," used by my boss in the executive coaching report. He was describing the impact of leadership on the members of the organization. Even though they were challenged by me at times and felt I was driven, they were compelled by my leadership approach.

When I first joined Performics as its CEO, the company was suffering from a tumultuous history. It had been bought, sold, and merged multiple times and was struggling with the transition from the Double-Click software technology that was retained by Google to a purely services company. The large media holding company Publicis Groupe had acquired the firm after Google had divested itself from the services side of the business because of an implied conflict of interest.

The employees of Performics had not fully grasped what this move into the holding company represented. I heard employees talk disdainfully about "marketing agencies." While I had empathy for the rocky history and acknowledged that the company's roots were firmly planted in technology, the fact of the matter was, as a company belonging to the third-largest media holding company in the world, Performics was now a marketing agency, whether they liked it or not.

My personal leadership approach was to combine tough love with genuine compassion. I communicated in an all-hands meeting that we were now an agency...period. It didn't matter if people weren't fond of it. This was the new reality that employees must accept. But, at the same time, I provided a vision for what Performics could become, demonstrating compassion and support in my words and actions. Not everyone agreed with me, but I made it clear this wasn't up for discussion, while providing hope and inspiration for the future.

I have come to understand that having Grit, while a necessary part of being a leader, does not always compel followers by itself. Combining Grace with Grit is better. An understanding and awareness of blending both are required for effective leadership and essential to understanding social dynamics in the workplace. This understanding and awareness are also essential to becoming a transformational leader.

Today's Broader Definition of Gender

I want to offer an important note about gender. Obviously the definition of gender is expansive today. After presentations about the concepts of Grace meets Grit, a number of men have approached me to share how they relate to and embody more Grace behaviors. By the same token, many women say they relate more to Grit when applying their personal leadership style.

My own research has determined that numerous leaders apply some attributes of both Grace and Grit leadership styles. This is good news!

The more we can discuss, understand, embrace, and value those differences and similarities, the faster we can move onto transformational leadership standards.

Workplace Impacts of Culture, Age, Geography

Beyond gender differences, communication styles are often influenced by other factors, including age, culture, and geography—to name a few. Each of these influences can be layered on top of gender differences and can have a meaningful effect on leadership behaviors. I want to acknowledge that these other factors exist and that they can, without question, affect workplace dynamics. However, they are not the focus of this book.

Identifying and establishing your communication preferences and using that information to analyze how your style may be affecting your performance in the workplace is important. As you become aware of typical male and female communication patterns, you will start noticing how your boss, your peers, and your employees blend Grace and Grit in their workplace personas, and you can use these new insights to improve communication and overall effectiveness within your organization. Remember, there is no wrong or right communication style. Each has its advantages and disadvantages.

Measuring Individuals by Leadership Behaviors

Behavioral theories of leadership focus on the study of specific actions of a leader. This is because leaders' behaviors are the best predictor of their leadership influences and, as a result, is the best determinant of leadership success. First developed by Robert Blake, this theoretical approach to understanding leaders creates categories of styles, which are aligned with the actions leaders may take, or the methods they use to reach their goals.[1]

Organizations look at leadership behaviors as a way to measure the current and future potential of employees. Tools, such as

DiSC, are also used to assess an individual's leadership behaviors as a means of predicting which behaviors individuals use naturally and which ones they don't. Companies develop a list of behaviors that they believe are most important to the organization. What often isn't discussed is the fact that, because of their differing approaches to communication, men and women often display widely different leadership behaviors.

In part 2, we explore more thoroughly how important decisive leadership behavior, for example, is for workplace executives. Experts agree that decision making might be perceived as the most important leadership behavior a person can possess in the workplace. Despite the agreed-upon significance, there are substantial biases about decision-making behaviors. The process of decision making can easily be misinterpreted because women and men use different approaches. Both are valid and add value to the organization, but because the organizational leadership standard is more often than not aligned to the Grit process, biased judgments occur.

The Most Biased Leadership Behavior

When making a decision, the Grace perspective is about including as many others in the process as possible. Conversely, the Grit perspective is to work independently. For Grit, sharing issues is simply wasted energy when the real focus should be on the immediate outcome. While Grace works diligently to ensure other voices are represented, Grit maintains status and efficiency during the process by directing others. And direction may not be limited to just followers; he may also directly instruct peers.

Leadership Behaviors and Communication Style

Leadership behavior is based on a communication or conversational style in which we share information with others through words, body language, and actions. Although we would all like to think that we are saying exactly what we mean, that's not always the case—especially when we are talking to someone who uses a communication style very different from our own. The subtle and not-so-subtle differences in communication styles can have a significant effect in situations when misunderstandings occur, assumptions are made, signals are missed, and wires are crossed as a consequence.

Let's examine the differences between the female communication style, which we'll embody as a character called "Grace," and the male communication style, which will be played by "Grit."

What Drives Women's Communication Style

For Grace, the entire focus and purpose of communicating, inside and outside of the workplace, is to establish and maintain relationships. All conversations occur with the intent to negotiate for closeness and to preserve intimacy. This is very different from Grit, who views conversations as a way to negotiate dominance and power and to achieve a tangible outcome. Grit experiences a world where conversations are negotiations made with the intent to achieve or maintain the dominant position against any attempts to usurp his rank.

What Drives Men's Communication Style

With his main focus on status and not as much on maintaining relationships, Grit can experience a disagreement with a colleague without suffering a significant negative impact on the overall relationship with that individual. Grace's complete focus on relationships means that a disruption can affect all interactions between involved individuals.

Several years ago, a woman approached me with a concern about a barrier that was preventing her team from accomplishing a goal. She described the barrier as an insurmountable disagreement over how to approach solving a problem. The problem itself was not the barrier; the disagreement was. She believed that this disagreement needed to be settled before the team could make any progress toward its goal. When I brought in her male counterpart to discuss the situation, he had no idea there was a barrier. He was, without her knowledge, moving actively toward a solution to the problem independently, completely unaware an issue existed that required attention.

Communication Style Differences, Nonverbal and Verbal

Communication and leadership style differences can also cause misunderstandings in nonverbal communication. Grace tends to nod her head to show she is listening and to express her acknowledgment that she understands. This nonverbal cue is a way of maintaining her connection to others. Grit may misinterpret this nodding as agreement, because he tends to nod only if he actually agrees with something. Grace could also misconstrue Grit's complete lack of head nodding as a signal that he is not listening.

Gender style differences are subtle, and many of us would like to believe that we are above these potential impediments to organizational harmony. Beyond the potential misunderstandings in a one-to-one setting, leadership behaviors also affect the relationship between leaders and followers. This is another area where Grit and Grace tend to have vast differences in their leadership approaches, and it's an area where Grace tends to shine.

How Relationship-Focused Leadership Benefits Organizations

Being in tune with interpersonal interactions, Grace values workplace interactions more than Grit. Research shows that female leaders tend to foster closer bonds with their followers compared with male leaders.[2] Women tend to base their leadership approach on the quality of interpersonal relationships between leaders and followers, so Grace is much more aware of the bonds she maintains with her followers. This relationship-oriented leadership style has characteristics that are more in tune with followers and indicates genuine concern about their well-being as well as their performance.[3] For Grace, forging and maintaining a strong bond with followers is considered essential, and these strong bonds are especially important when someone is leading followers through organizational change.

In my own personal experience, I have found that defining the direction (instilling the company vision) is the easy part of leadership. The more difficult task is persuading others to journey there with you. Getting people moving in the right direction is a lot easier when you understand how they genuinely feel and have a deep emotional connection with them.

Leadership Research Assessment Firm Zenger and Folkman collected 360-degree feedback data from forty-five thousand leaders in a number of organizations around the world and found that women excel in a variety of leadership competencies over men, especially in the relationship-focused areas commonly attributed to Grace. Women scored higher on integrity and honesty, developing others, inspiring and motivating others, building relationships, collaboration, and teamwork.[4]

Gender Differences in Early Childhood

Deborah Tannen maintains that relationship gender differences begin at an early age, with boys and girls spending most of their time playing in same-sex groups. Though some of the activities are similar, the games groups of boys play differ from those girls play, the ways that language is used within the games differs, and the role of status within play is vastly different.[5]

According to Tannen, boys tend to play outside in large groups that are hierarchically structured. These groups have a clearly established leader who tells others what to do and how to do it and who resists what other boys propose. Individuals negotiate status by giving orders and making them stick. Boys' games have winners and losers and elaborate systems of rules that are frequently the subject of arguments. Finally, boys are frequently heard boasting about their skills and arguing about who is best.

Girls, on the other hand, have a very different approach to playing. They often play in small groups or pairs, with a best friend in the center of a girl's life, according to Tannen. Within a group or while playing in pairs, girls' primary goal is to build and maintain intimacy. There are no winners or losers—even for outdoor activities where everyone has a turn, such as jump rope.

I can remember playing outdoors for hours with a friend as a child. We spent our time acting the parts of favorite television characters and took turns playing the part of the key character, often Daniel Boone. Neither of us wanted to play the part of Daniel's wife, Rebecca, but we dutifully each took turns playing the part to be fair to one another. Girls tend to make suggestions instead of giving orders, which are more likely to be accepted by other girls. Being liked and preserving the relationship are the goals of play, not hierarchy or status, and a tangible goal or outcome is rarely involved. I never thought about what the outcome of playing Daniel Boone all day would be—it was about the experience and sharing it with my friend.

Understanding the Status-Oriented Approach

As a leader, I have struggled at times with the nuances of the status-oriented, competitive approach favored by men. I can remember attending a meeting at Twitter where a Sales leader met with the leader of the Engineering Department to solve an employee-resource issue.

The Sales lead led the meeting and kicked it off by saying the following: "I am so, so sorry that we f—ed this up. I know what it's like. I had this happen to me before. It happened on our side because the manager of this team is on leave and the person overseeing the process was not watching it closely."

None of this was actually true, except for the fact that there was a person on leave. Both teams had engaged in a number of conversations with the senior Engineering lead. The Sales lead went on to stress why alignment was so important and then shifted gears and focused on why this particular project was so important to his department. He said he had asked for resources from Engineering many times in the past, but that department had declined the request, so Sales felt the need to hire its own resources.

At this point the Sales lead turned the meeting over to the Engineering lead, who opened his argument with a derogatory comment about everyone in the company except his department. He and the Sales lead went back and forth in a series of veiled threats and mysterious posturing. Finally, fifty minutes into the meeting, their interactions indicated they had reached a vague agreement. Others in the room remained confused, and discussions followed the meeting in which others wondered if anything had been accomplished. The negotiating men, however, seemed content with the outcome.

I walked away from this experience feeling perplexed. Despite having more than twenty years of work experience, I completely missed most of the political nuances of this interaction and left the meeting wondering how effective I would have been had I been expected to lead the negotiations using this approach. Instead of beginning the meeting with vague apologies and condolences, I would have openly laid out the business problem, honestly and transparently. I would have then requested the team come together to devise a solution. My approach would have been to avoid any posturing or veiled communications.

Would that have been effective? I will never know.

Grit's strategy of instructing and giving information rather than asking questions or consulting with others is a way of establishing and maintaining status. In the Twitter example, the Sales and Engineering leads had an interchange that involved alternately telling and acquiescing, resulting in a mysterious dance involving status and actions. Each director wanted to get his way and not lose his position. The openly competitive and hierarchy-focused references reminded everyone who was in charge.

As Tannen describes this behavior, boys monitor their relations for subtle shifts in status by keeping track of who's giving orders and who's taking them. This is very different from girls, who monitor their friendships for subtle shifts in alliances.

Organizations' Comfort with Male Leadership Style

Often the Grit leadership approach is the style organizations find most comfortable. Talent Innovations analyzed the 360-degree feedback results of nearly fourteen thousand leaders and managers in the United Kingdom to ascertain how men and women rate against eighteen leadership competencies. Men consistently scored higher in thinking about the big picture, managing financial impacts, driving improved business results, making a strong first impression, expressing views with confidence, and being visible across the organization.[6] Is this because of Grit's focus on status and achieving immediate tangible outcomes? Remember that, at the senior leadership level, in most cases men are dealing with other men, and speaking the language of Grit is helpful when that is the corporate norm.

Another study performed by the Management Research Group indicated that men rate higher on competencies such as business aptitude, financial understanding, and big-picture perspective. They also scored higher on strategic planning, persuading, delegating, and being more reserved in expression. These attributes seem to reinforce male leadership dominance as an accepted leadership style more than demonstrating competency distinctions favoring actual performance. Men and women scored equally well on effective thinking, credibility with peers and followers, effective use of resources, willingness to listen, customer relations, team performance, and overall effectiveness.[7]

The question is less about actual competency and more about whether or not companies are ready to change the leadership standard in their organizations. A recent study found that 80 percent of respondents believe both women and men make equally good leaders, but only 43 percent felt that businesses are ready to hire women for top executive positions.[8]

We have already established that Grace-focused executives tend to gravitate toward the tenants of transformational leadership. On the other hand, Grit leaders tend to use a more traditional, transactional style of leadership. Transactional leadership is about an "if, then" exchange of rewards based on behaviors. Despite research that demonstrates the greater effectiveness of the transformational leadership style, the control and command method used by Grit is still alive and well and accepted as the norm in the corporate world today. As the Twitter example affirms, having some recognition and understanding of the Grit approach can be beneficial in specific work situations.

If I had hijacked the Twitter meeting and used a more transformational leadership approach to solving the Sales–Engineering problem, what would have happened? Would the Sales lead have interrupted me and taken over the meeting, driving it back to a more comfortable place? This is what I suspect would have happened. The less comfortable, transformational approach likely would have been considered ineffective.

To make matters even more complicated, I have seen the same Sales lead behave as a transformational leader. In fact, I would argue that it was his dominant style of leadership, but he adjusted his approach to fit the situation. He understood what type of leadership style was required to dominate his adversary, which in this case was the Engineering lead. Because of prescriptive and descriptive biases, women have less latitude in adapting their leadership style, and they are far more comfortable using the transformational approach.

In organizations where women are represented in a leadership team, transformational leadership is likely already being practiced. This is great for organizations that recognize the benefit of this progressive leadership style and are seeking leaders who are skilled in it, but this style is often not recognized consciously or valued by leadership teams.

Throughout my career I have often asked myself, "How can I, along with other women, get more Grit?" Or, at the very least, how can we be better prepared about what to expect from Grit and have a greater understanding of those behaviors, so we are more comfortable in situations like the one I experienced at Twitter. The goal is to embrace more Grit without compromising the natural and, some would say, superior transformational leadership skills that emerge from Grace.

The Value of Transformational Leaders

The overwhelming research regarding how women naturally possess and effectively apply the attributes of transformational leadership has already been established, and having these innate skills and abilities will become even more important in the workplace in the future. Transformational leadership is also the key to getting more women into leadership positions, because those who adopt this style are better accepted in the majority of organizations.

A Caliper study found that employees who worked for a group of female transformational leaders were intellectually stimulated. They also found this group of women leaders was good for the business in general. They were creative problem solvers, were motivated and resilient, and had the ability to perceive and respond to the needs of the team.[9]

Because the corporate standard for leadership behaviors is still modeled after the control-and command methods, men have more freedom to exercise a broad range of styles without receiving negative feedback. Men do not have to prove their leadership competency as often as women. A man's legitimacy in the role is already assumed, because it is more consistent with gender stereotyping.[10] As a result, men more often can use a variety of leadership styles: transactional, laissez-faire, and transformational, sometimes interchangeably and almost always with success. Men also have been known to apply a blended style called "transformational-transactional" leadership. This is a "give and take" working relationship in which the rapport between leader and follower is established through a rewards system for meeting specific objectives.

Blending Leadership Styles: Grace Meets Grit

The real opportunity for women is to effectively blend Grace and Grit. We all understand that accomplishing this is perhaps easier said than actually done—especially when there is a well-documented double standard for women who actively demonstrate more Grit. There are undisputable gender biases that women will continue to face. These are deeply ingrained and will take a long time to shift.

The backlash from these biases doesn't always come from men. In fact, embracing more Grit means being willing to violate the underlying traditional principles that guide our behaviors and violate the Grace rules of relationship-focused engagement. There are also cultural barriers that contribute to this complicated subject.

I was reminded of this when I volunteered as a senior woman leader to work with a number of young women engineers at Twitter. The goal was to help them put their performance review feedback into measurable actions. While this sounds really simple, I found it to be quite difficult in practice. Imagine receiving feedback such as, "I want you to be more visible." Most of us might be confused about the intent behind this criticism. More specific direction is required to formulate an action plan. What I didn't realize until I was in the room with these women, who comprised just 3 percent of the Engineering population, was that they were not only viewing the feedback through a gender lens, but most of them were from Asia and, in some cases, English was a second language.

Dissecting the definition of "visible" was additionally challenging, given those cultural and language hurdles. The bottom line is that, for women to be more successful in leadership positions and to fully embrace Grace and Grit, both men and women will need to have a better understanding of our differences and strengths in a way that enables all of us to color outside the traditional lines.

Leadership Behaviors and the Three Leadership Styles

Leadership unquestionably matters. Research has demonstrated leadership effectiveness correlates positively to positive organizational performance.[11] Good leaders have a positive effect on their followers and the overall performance of an organization.

As I progressed in my career from individual contributor to first-time manager, to team manager, and so on, I gradually developed my own personal leadership style. I created my distinct leadership brand by adopting a style that fit my personality, was modeled after the best attributes I had observed in other leaders I admired, and was centered on organizational values and norms. This process naturally involved a lot of trial and error.

Individual leadership behaviors, such as acting decisively and confidently, were always a development area that had high priority for me. I understood that others' perceptions of those behaviors were important to my individual growth and career success. However, I did not spend any time or energy studying the individual types of leadership styles.

Until I began my research into leadership for *Grace Meets Grit*, I was not aware that there are three primary styles of leadership, nor did I understand which style fit with my own leadership brand.

The Transactional Style

In the 1980s, researcher Bernard M. Bass developed what is referred to today as Bass's Leadership Theory, which describes the specific behaviors composing each of three leadership styles: transactional, laissez-faire, and transformational.[12]

Transactional leadership is the most traditional and managerial style of leadership, and despite a gradual shift toward the transformational style, it is still the leadership style most often practiced in corporate America. Transactional leaders focus on supervision, organization, and group performance. They gain compliance from their followers through rewards and punishments. This is what leadership experts tend to call the "give and take" of the transactional style. Quite simply, if followers do as instructed, they are rewarded for that behavior.

Transactional leaders tend to be directive, and action oriented, which is a natural fit for leaders inclined toward Grit behaviors. The transactional style is defined by two dimensions, according to Bass's theory. The first dimension is "contingent reward," where leaders provide rewards to their followers for meeting their expectations. Rewards are often tangible, such as trips or bonuses.

The second dimension is "management by exception," where leaders maintain the status quo, intervene when subordinates do not meet acceptable performance levels, and initiate corrective action to improve performance. "Punishment" can take a number of forms, including withholding praise, attention, or promotions, or more punitive actions.

Transactional leaders who actively manage have a tendency toward "micro-managing," or supervising by closely monitoring every step their followers take toward achieving a milestone. Some transactional leaders practice a more passive approach and tend to be completely disconnected from their followers until there is an urgent problem. I have worked with both active and passive transactional leaders and have found that each can be frustrating in their own way. A sure sign that you are working for a transactional leader is that the goal of your work becomes limited to keeping the leader happy, rather than having a more meaningful, higher objective. This is what limits the potential of transactional leadership. It fails to tap into the spirit and soul of the followers and harness that energy for the benefit of the entire organization.

The Laissez-Faire Style

The second style of leadership is laissez-faire, which generally refers to a leader who is completely passive in his management approach. Leaders who adopt this style are entirely hands-off and allow group members to make the decisions. Researchers have found that this is generally the leadership style that leads to the lowest productivity among group members; however, it can be effective when the individual is leading a team of very senior and highly experienced people.[13]

My own experience working for a leader using the laissez-faire approach is that it works well for individuals who enjoy autonomy and are comfortable working without leadership support. Success in this case often requires having a good relationship with leaders above the passive manager. If senior sponsorship is required for individual and team success, having a checked-out manager can be frustrating at the least, and can endanger effectiveness at the worst. The bottom line: a manager who is out of touch with the team and the projects usually lacks the connection with followers required to deliver optimal performance.

The Transformational Style

Transformational leadership is the third leadership style and the most progressive of the three. Leadership expert and presidential biographer James MacGregor Burns popularized the transformational leadership concept in 1978. According to Burns, it is when "leaders and followers make each other advance to a higher level of moral and motivation."[14] The power of transformational leaders comes from their ability to stimulate and inspire others to produce exceptional work. This is in contrast to the transactional style of leadership, where motivation is extrinsic and encourages minimal compliance for meeting particular objectives.

Through the strength of their vision and personality, transformational leaders are able to inspire followers to change their expectations, perceptions, and motivations and to work toward common goals. Transformational leaders not only inspire their followers but also challenge, engage, develop, and align them. As a result, followers trust, admire, and respect their leader and tend to be more loyal to their organization.

Transformational leadership is correlated to more positive organizational outcomes than any other leadership style. Women leaders typically outscore males on applying the measures of transformational leadership,[15] and research has shown that women who adopt this style tend to have better success in progressing in leadership positions.

Bernard Bass, in his own research, built on Burns's initial concept of transformational leadership. He affirmed the importance of the follower/leader relationship, saying transformational leadership can be defined on the basis of the impact that it has on followers. Transformational leaders, he suggested, garner trust, respect, and admiration from their followers.

Bass expanded on the original definition by establishing four dimensions to this style of leadership, sometimes referred to as the four *I*'s: idealized influence, inspirational motivation, individualized consideration, and intellectual stimulation. Many leadership experts have built on the four *I*'s theory over the years. Let's examine each of the *I*'s and how leaders can apply these behaviors to their personal leadership style.

Idealized Influence

"Idealized influence" means the leader serves as a role model for followers and authentically demonstrates leadership through his or her own actions. The notion of "actions speaking louder than words" is the best way to describe idealized influence. Transformational leaders do not believe that their status enables them to behave in a privileged way that is different from what is expected from their followers. This quality is also sometimes described as "charisma." Charismatic or inspirational leaders also tend to display conviction, take stands, and appeal to followers on an emotional level. They are not afraid of demonstrating their emotions and passion, and tend to be mindful of how their actions impact their followers.

Inspirational Motivation

Transformational leaders apply "inspirational motivation" to incentivize their followers. They can be cheerleaders of sorts, both for individual and team accomplishments. These leaders clearly articulate a vision that is appealing and inspiring to followers. Leaders who possess inspirational motivation challenge followers by demanding high standards, communicating optimism about the future and goal attainment, and provide meaning for the immediate tasks at hand. This inspirational vision is often communicated in multiple formats—broadly through more choreographed presentations that inspire the entire organization and through individual interactions in which followers are able to make a personal connection with leaders.

Individualized Consideration

A transformational leader demonstrates "individualized consideration," a genuine concern for the needs and feelings of followers. These leaders are personally invested in the development of their followers and often serve as mentors and coaches. They take into account individual needs and desires within a group. This personal attention is a key element in optimizing employee performance by attending to followers' needs.

Again, actions are exceptionally important, as followers will decide if the leader truly cares about them as individuals or if they are unknown, invisible, and unimportant. One of my favorite professors in college learned every single student's name, despite the fact that he had more than one hundred students in his class. I was impressed when he called me by name outside of class, and I truly believed he cared about how well I did and would know if I didn't do well. Consequently, I worked harder and had perfect attendance in his classes compared with other classes, where I felt invisible.

Intellectual Stimulation

The transformational leader uses "intellectual stimulation" by challenging followers to be innovative and creative, and to constantly reach for a higher level of performance through a commonly shared purpose. This is likely where the "transformational" name came from. As a result, followers strive to reach higher levels of efficacy and to better themselves individually, which has a positive effect on the organization as a whole.

Transformational Leadership and the HP Way

Coming up through the ranks at Hewlett-Packard, I learned about leadership through a culture that valued its employees as the company's greatest resource. When I joined the organization in 1992, I was introduced to the famous set of corporate values, the HP Way. More than just a management philosophy ahead of its time, the HP Way set the tone for how employees worked together and how leaders influenced followers. This unique leadership style arguably distinguished the company more than any of its products. The HP Way included respect for the individual, responsibility to the communities in which the company operates, and a deeply held belief that profit is not the fundamental goal of the company.

I have checked in with several friends who still work at HP, and, sadly, they claim that the HP Way is only occasionally used today and was largely lost due to repeated revisions by a succession of leaders who had not personally lived it. Today, the HP culture is also less homogeneous because of several large mergers. However, many key behaviors of the HP Way (including trust, teamwork, and respect) are still deeply embedded in the culture and continue to affect daily interactions in a positive way. The HP Way affected me so deeply that I have kept the handbook that outlined the five key principles. I now recognize that transformational leadership is represented in each of these five value statements.

The HP Way

We have trust and respect for individuals. We approach each situation with the belief that people want to do a good job and will do so, given the proper tools and support. We attract highly capable, diverse, innovative people and recognize their efforts and contributions to the company. HP people contribute enthusiastically and share in the success that they make possible.

We focus on a high level of achievement and contribution. Our customers expect HP products and services to be of the highest quality and to provide lasting value. To achieve this, all HP people, especially managers, must be leaders who generate enthusiasm and respond with extra effort to meet customer needs. Techniques and management practices that are effective today may be outdated in the future. For us to remain at the forefront in all our activities, people should always be looking for new and better ways to do their work.

We conduct our business with uncompromising integrity. We expect HP people to be open and honest in their dealings to earn the trust and loyalty of others. People at every level are expected to adhere to the highest standards of business ethics and must understand that anything less is unacceptable. As a practical matter, ethical conduct cannot be assured by written HP policies and codes; it must be an integral part of the organization, a deeply ingrained tradition that is passed from one generation of employees to another.

We achieve our common objectives through teamwork. We recognize that it is only through effective cooperation within and among organizations that we can achieve our goals. Our commitment is to work as a worldwide team to fulfill the expectations of our customers, shareholders and others who depend upon us. The benefits and obligations of doing business are shared among all HP people.

> **We encourage flexibility and innovation.** We create an inclusive work environment that supports the diversity of our people and stimulates innovation. We strive for overall objectives that are clearly stated and agreed upon, and allow people flexibility in working toward goals in ways that they help determine are best for the organization. HP people should personally accept responsibility and be encouraged to upgrade their skills and capabilities through ongoing training and development. This is especially important in a technical business, where the rate of progress is rapid and where people are expected to adapt to change.[16]

Even though I have not been an HP employee for nearly a decade, I still find the values of the HP Way ring true as core components in my individual leadership style and approach. Now that I understand more about the different styles of leadership, I recognize that I learned how to be a transformational leader through the application of the HP Way, as I "grew up" within a culture that expected its leaders to behave this way. It was the only style that I knew. It was how I expected leaders to behave, and it was admired throughout the world as a leadership model, so I adopted it as my own. I found that it worked well for me and for the teams and organizations I led. The HP Way embodies Grace qualities. It acknowledges that people and relationships should be at the core of how a company behaves with customers, partners and employees.

Women's Application of Transformational Leadership

Women are natural transformational leaders. In a meta-analysis of forty-five studies comparing men and women leaders, women were found to be stronger in three of the four transformational dimensions: inspirational motivation, intellectual stimulation, and individual consideration.[17]

By comparison, the same study indicated that male leaders were more likely than females to exhibit transactional leadership, in particular management-by-exception and laissez-faire leadership.

Recent research has also shown that women apply five of the eight transformational behaviors that have been found to improve organizational performance more often than their male counterparts: people development, expectations and rewards, role modeling, inspiration, and participative decision-making.

Women and men apply two behaviors equally: intellectual stimulation and efficient communications. Men apply only two behaviors more often than women: making decisions based on the individual and taking control and corrective action.[18]

Additional Benefits of Transformational Leadership

Research has also shown that women who display more transformational behaviors in the workplace are more likely to have success in rising through the leadership ranks. Specifically, the "individualized consideration" dimension of transformational leadership has proven to be particularly effective for women seeking promotion to senior management positions.[19] Individuals who seek to rise through the leadership ranks require support at all levels of the organization, thus the skill of connecting with colleagues above, below, and laterally is a key to success in leadership roles. It is interesting to note that those women who choose to adopt more traditional transactional or laissez-faire approaches to leadership have less success in progressing through the management ranks.

Beyond the positive organizational benefits, transformational leadership has become a hot topic of late in leadership and management discussions because research indicates that this style of leadership is most effective for attracting and retaining millennials.

Attracting and Retaining Millennials

Millennials are the generation of people born between 1982 and 2003, the largest generation of people in history. By 2020, 86 million millennials will be in the workplace. This will represent 40 percent of the working population. Needless to say, understanding what motivates millennials in their place of work is becoming critically important for organizations globally.

Today's employers describe millennials as a group who have strong opinions and, as such, already have a reputation for being a difficult talent segment for companies to manage. From my own personal experience, they are known for being unwilling to work for organizations that exercise a leadership style that is inconsistent with their own set of values.

The Intelligence Group, an organization that studies millennials, has found they also have high career aspirations and specific expectations about their leadership preferences:

- Seventy-two percent would like to be their own boss.
- Seventy-nine percent want their boss to act more like a coach or mentor.
- Eighty-eight percent prefer to work in a collaborative culture rather than a competitive one.
- Seventy-four percent desire flexible work schedules.
- Eighty-eight percent want work–life integration, which differs from work–life balance, because they believe work and life blend together inextricably.[20]

Additional research indicates that 88 percent of millennials tend to have greater engagement when working in an organization that has a more inclusive leadership style.[21] In an interview with Kathy Caprino for *Forbes* magazine, Medtronic CEO Bill George was quoted as saying, "The hierarchical style of leadership that was prevalent in the 1980s and 1990s will not work today . . . Millennials work well in empowering, collaborative environments where outcomes are much more important than who gets credit."[22]

Given the importance of keeping employees engaged, organizations are beginning to understand the necessity of hiring and nurturing leaders who understand how to get the most out of their employees. Millennials crave a transformational leadership environment, and women, with their inclination to lead through relationship-building behaviors, are well suited to creating this workplace of the future.

Judging Women by Traditional Traits

Given all the data on women's innate capacity to exercise transformational leadership, why are women still largely missing from the leadership ranks today? Though women appear to apply transformational leadership behaviors more, research on stereotypes about men, women, and leaders has shown that traits associated with the prototypical leader (such as decision making, driving for results, confidence, and power) are considered, stereotypically, to be more masculine.

Because of this, male leaders do not need to prove their competency in the same manner that women do. Their legitimacy in a leadership role is already assumed because the male style is more consistent with the behaviors associated with leaders. This is likely why men can adopt other, less effective leadership styles, such as transactional or laissez-faire, despite the fact that these styles are not as likely to produce positive workplace outcomes as leadership styles associated with women.

All of this information may shed light on why women, more often than men, find the transition into management particularly confusing and painful. As a new manager, a woman may still be formulating her individual leadership style. Modeling her style after male peers and managers may actually prove to be undesirable when it comes to advancement potential. At the same time, men may measure a woman's leadership style against their own style even if that style is not effective.

Despite the progress women have made over the last several decades in moving into more managerial positions, these expectations about gender in terms of leadership behaviors and styles persist. Even though women naturally apply the transformational leadership style, they are assumed to be not as qualified for leadership positions. This is why a discussion about the next level of leadership behaviors, in addition to the overarching leadership style, is necessary. To make progress, we must have a deeper understanding of the value of having a diverse perspective represented in the behaviors that we explore in part 2.

Measuring Employees by Leadership Behaviors

Organizations, including corporations, have a long list of leadership behaviors that are desirable in seeking to gain a competitive advantage. Various entities have identified the behaviors that are most desirable in leaders, and individual organizations have established sets of behaviors that they feel are most suitable for employees working in a particular environment. There are even unique sets of behaviors that have been designated as most desired for specific situations, such as vital behaviors in a time of crisis, or those most valuable in building a start-up.

All employees are measured on their leadership behaviors. And leadership styles, behaviors, skills, and abilities are, of course, intertwined. Individual behaviors, such as being able to inspire employees, being strongly driven to produce results, or having confidence, add up to form the basis of a person's leadership style.

Leadership behaviors are important because, as individual qualities, they are not reserved exclusively for managers or leaders. Each contributor within a company is evaluated on their leadership behaviors. When describing an individual employee's performance, leaders use leadership behaviors to make their assessments. For example, an employee might be described as "an effective decision-maker; she drives for results without allowing barriers to get in her way." Beyond performance evaluations, job descriptions also contain desired leadership-behavior attributes, such as "seeking a results-driven, inspirational individual who is decisive."

Understanding the differences in the way women and men apply individual behaviors is critical for every person, because competencies in these behaviors are evaluated throughout an individual's career. It's also important to note that biases associated with these behaviors tend to become more important as a person's role increasingly becomes visible to the organization, and may even become barriers for individuals, preventing them from progressing in their career journey.

When we embrace differences in leadership behaviors, acknowledging the fact that men and women think and act differently in the workplace because they are fundamentally different, Grace and Grit can work together more effectively. Having different leadership styles and approaches to solving workplace situations is a good thing. Diversity brings value to individuals, teams, and organizations alike. I hope that, as we explore individual behaviors, meaningful conversations will begin. We will all be happier and have better organizational outcomes when Grace meets Grit.

PART II

The Leadership Behaviors

A number of years ago when I was just starting out as a people manager, I had one of my first experiences as a leadership coach. There was a woman on my team who had a particularly unusual set of leadership skills. On the one hand, she was extremely creative, in fact talented enough that she created and sold her own artwork for fun. Her creative skills were valuable to the organization and to the team because she was constantly innovating and inspiring the team to reach new heights.

On the other hand, she was equally very analytical, liked regimented processes, and was meticulous in detailed follow-through. This blend of creative and analytical skills was what made her a particularly valuable member of the team. Not only was she able to generate new ideas, but she had the discipline and understanding to execute those ideas and would often put sophisticated processes in place along the way that helped the organization to be more efficient and effective overall.

However, under stress, her behavior would change dramatically toward her analytical set of skills. As a leadership coach, I find it to be quite normal for an individual's behavior tendencies to shift under pressure, though some people have more dramatic shifts than others. In this particular case, the behavior shift from creating to analyzing had a less than positive effect on many of her leadership behaviors, including interacting with her team and, ultimately, her overall effectiveness.

At the time, I did not have years of coaching experience or even a very good set of tools to help her understand the impact of her shifting behaviors. In fact, I wasn't aware at all that leadership behaviors constituted a discipline (branch of knowledge). The woman in question wanted to improve, so together we worked through recognition of the behaviors and implemented a personal-development plan. Through awareness and a plan, she was able to leverage her strengths and improve her leadership capabilities.

After years of coaching others and my own self-development work, I have come to recognize that refining leadership behaviors, in myself and in others, is the key to improved effectiveness, both for individuals and teams. Examining leadership qualities through the lens of gender differences is a valuable component of understanding and building leadership behaviors. Leadership behaviors are the measuring stick used by others to determine if we have the potential to lead and if we are effective in our role.

As a leadership coach, I use quantitative assessments to determine innate behavior tendencies. I also gather feedback from others to better understand that leader's effectiveness. Assessing behaviors is also used in the performance-review process, as understanding them can help improve team effectiveness. Organizations determine which behaviors employees need to have to deliver the best results and which fit within the organization's culture.

As a coach, I help individuals understand where their strengths lie and the areas where they have growth opportunities. While leaders may never excel in some areas, having an awareness of our strengths *and* our weaknesses helps us to become better leaders. Rarely is a leader outstanding in every category.

Despite the obvious significance surrounding leadership behaviors in the workplace and the amount of time and energy spent on them, I have seldom seen these behaviors examined from a gender perspective. The differences in how men and women respectively demonstrate leadership qualities may seem subtle and are often overlooked. Consequently, misunderstandings occur, judgments are made, and opportunities are lost—all having a negative effect on workplace effectiveness. To change gender dynamics in the workplace, we need to understand the impact of gender on leadership behaviors.

Companies use a long list of leadership behaviors to analyze leadership effectiveness. Consulting firms have rated these behaviors from most important to least. Others claim there are five to ten critical qualities leaders need to drive organizational performance. The six behaviors I chose to focus on in this book—inspiring, decisive, driven, confident, powerful, and resilient—are the qualities often associated with successful male leaders. My belief is that women leaders can bring their special superpower, relationship acumen, to each of these vital behaviors, which will add significant value to their organizations. In many cases, these talents lie beneath the surface or their value is misunderstood or not considered a priority by women. Embracing all six leadership behaviors can make the difference between a good leader and a remarkable one.

At the end of each chapter in part 2 is the story of an inspiring woman leader in history who embodies the behavior on which that chapter focuses. Also at the end of each chapter is a practical reference guide to building each critical quality in your own leadership style, from both a Grace and a Grit perspective.

CHAPTER 4

Inspiring

I could feel my heart beating in my throat as I considered the choices listed on the sheet of paper below, the pen gripped tightly in my right hand. Uncharacteristically, my entire hand was shaking, my heart was pounding, and I felt a little light-headed. I took a deep breath. The oxygen sent a calming wave through my body, down my limbs to calm my shaking fingers. My pen was paused above an application that I had, thus far, rapidly completed until I reached a question with a response containing three boxes. Here, I was asked to choose one of the following: "clothed," "semi-nude," or "nude."

My pen suddenly sped into action and I chose "clothed." Instantly I felt a rush of guilt and a little remorse soaking through my rapidly slipping confidence. I stopped to ask myself, "What is semi-nude? Should I choose it instead? Is that a safe option?"

I had mental images associated with each category. I ignored them and moved on to the next section. Apparently, there was no going back to "nude."

The form was almost complete when the photographer slapped my knee with the palm of his hand as he passed by the tiny stool I was perched on to complete my application. I nearly tipped off sideways.

"Need some water, honey?" he asked without looking at my face. I nodded. My throat felt suddenly bone dry, as if I had been walking through the desert for weeks. I was ashamed that he seemed to sense my apprehension. I told myself it was only anxiety, that I didn't believe in fear. I checked in with myself, gathered my courage, and reaffirmed my determination to really go through with this—even "clothed."

It was May of 1985. I was just beginning my sophomore year at Oregon State University (OSU) and working full time as a reporter for the university newspaper, the *Daily Barometer*. The woman who was the editor of the *Barometer* had discovered that *Playboy* magazine had come to our small college town of Corvallis, Oregon, seeking out potential models for the upcoming "Girls of the Pac 10" issue, which features women from the Pacific 10 collegiate athletic conference.

I could have chosen to just interview the photographer, but instead I had opted to put myself through the tryout process to experience first-hand what it was like to audition for the notorious magazine. The end result would be a story in the *Daily Barometer* about my trying out, so all university women could share in this uncommon experience. If I were to be chosen, I had no intention of actually going all the way through the process and posing like the other young women who would actually appear in the Pac 10 issue.

When the photographer turned his full attention to me, after making some adjustments to his camera, he requested I "pose," and my immediate reaction was to freeze. What the hell did "pose" mean? Before I had time to overthink the request and evolve into a second round of panic, he guided me through the steps of "posing."

As he instructed me to "put your hands in your pockets," "tilt your head," I felt my confidence return and remembered why I was here. This was a very personal assignment for me, and it meant much more than just reporting a story for the newspaper. It was about being courageous enough to walk in the shoes of someone who was, for me and so many others, an inspirational legend—Gloria Steinem.

Before making the decision to sit in that room and bravely face the photographer, I had reread Steinem's undercover story, "A Bunny's Tale," which was published in the May and June 1963 issues of *Show* magazine. I was born in 1965, so I grew up reading another magazine, *Ms.*, long before I even knew about Steinem's undercover experience with the Playboy Club.

The timing of the publication of "A Bunny's Tale" couldn't have been more ideal: it was the same year that Betty Friedan's book *The Feminine Mystique* and Sylvia Plath's *The Bell Jar* were published. It was a powerful time for women. The feminist movement was gaining momentum throughout the country, and Steinem's undercover prose complemented the efforts of Friedan and Plath perfectly. Reading about Friedan, Plath, and Steinem many years after the movement's heyday had influenced my own journalistic pursuits and unabashed public embrace of feminism, despite the fact that the popularity of the feminist movement had faded by the time I was old enough to understand what one was.

The foundational premise of "A Bunny's Tale" was that the sexual revolution would fail if men were the only ones permitted to shape it. Gloria Steinem was determined to inspire women to define their own sexual present and future. She exposed how one powerful man, Hugh Hefner, was attempting to do it for them. In taking on the *Playboy* magazine founder and his Playboy Clubs, Steinem demonstrated the power that a single individual can have even when up against an opponent as formidable as Hefner and his mighty media empire.

Steinem's storytelling methodology was consistent with the 1960s' journalistic style of employing factual and raw personal experiences to deliver a powerful, more relevant, and authentically persuasive account. This is what inspired me to go undercover and ultimately publish my own personal story about posing, albeit fully clothed, for *Playboy* in the OSU *Daily Barometer*.

By emulating the person who motivated me and participating with my own individual story, I had become part of something much larger. Steinem had inspired me to join a movement, and she did so leading by example. Her passion and commitment caused me to choose an experience that stimulated unexpected personal growth, and, through that experience, I transcended beyond the boundaries I had set for myself. This is what inspirational leaders do.

Traits of an Inspiring Leader

I am fortunate to have had a number of inspirational leaders throughout my career. The skill of inspiring followers through personal charisma is arguably a very important leadership characteristic. How many truly charismatic leaders exist? It is the quality that powerfully separates the most effective leaders from the average and least effective leaders.

Inspirational leaders share many qualities with transformational leaders. I believe inspirational leadership is actually about relationships and intrinsically motivating others, which are skills associated with Grace. Even those who are not innately charismatic can leverage strong relationship skills to inspire others.

Of the eight transformational leadership behaviors that improve organizational performance, five fall under the umbrella of inspirational leadership: inspiring others into action, people development, expectations and rewards, role modeling, and participative decision-making. According to a Harvard Business School study in which fifty thousand leaders were assessed by approximately a half-million colleagues, leaders who have the ability to inspire create the highest levels of employee engagement and commitment, and "inspiring" is the factor most people name when asked what qualities they would most like a leader to possess.[1]

But what does it mean to be inspiring? Researchers at the University of Michigan and Catalyst, a nonprofit organization whose mission is to accelerate progress for women through workplace inclusion, developed a definition that I believe encompasses the breadth of this transformational leadership behavior: motivating others toward greater enthusiasm and commitment to work by appealing to emotion and values, and leading by personal example.[2]

To hone in on how leaders become inspirational, Harvard searched its database for those leaders who received the highest scores on the competency of "inspires and motivates to high performance." The university found approximately one thousand leaders who fit the criteria. These leaders were then analyzed for what they did that separated them from their less-inspiring counterparts.

According to the *Harvard Business Review*, the data indicated that some of what inspiring leaders did was specific and tangible—and also consistent with transformational leaders. For example, inspirational leaders set stretch goals with their team. They spent time personally developing their followers. They engaged in highly collaborative behaviors and encouraged those around them to be more innovative.

Examples of making emotional connections with followers meant they were better at establishing a clear vision, more effective in their overall communications, and willing to spend more time actively communicating about their vision. They were also passionate champions of organizational change and perceived as effective role models within the organization. Finally, the data indicated that leaders who possessed more of these behaviors collectively—meaning the more of these behaviors a leader exhibited, the more inspirational the leader was perceived to be—experienced a cumulative effect.

Readily Sharing Information

I can remember, early in my career, recognizing that one of the main sources of power was information. The individuals possessing the greatest amount of information had the most power. This was primarily because information was limited to only a few individuals, and there were fewer information sources and distribution methods. As a consequence, information was tightly held and controlled, and therefore harder to come by. Those who had it were the ones others looked to for guidance, because they were considered to be part of the inside circle. First in the Information Age, and unquestionably now in the Participation Age, companies are envisioning a different corporate culture by actively seeking out leaders who have an authentic, transparent communication style and are comfortable with openly sharing information—at all levels.

Being Naturally Open, Transparent, and Authentic

The good news is this type of open, transparent, and authentic leadership style is often more inherent in women who lead than in male leaders. For me, being a CEO was not about a title or having information, knowledge, or power that others did not have. It was about empowering others, rather than holding power and authority *over* others. We return to this idea in chapter 8, on the powerful behavior.

A remarkable, inspirational leader motivates others to take action. Inspiring leaders pursue leadership goals beyond the immediate and short term and embody a humble personal perspective accompanied by a fierce desire for the organization's success. Through their actions, more than their words, they help to create a culture bigger than themselves to ensure that the organization endures well beyond their own personal leadership tenure.

Having the Power to Ignite Collaboration

Researchers John Zenger and Joseph Folkman conducted a multi-year research project detailed in their book *The Extraordinary Leader*.[3] They examined more than two hundred thousand surveys for twenty thousand leaders for whom the researchers had correlated company performance data. The researchers reported two factors that they found distinguished the best leaders from the worst: they inspire individuals to achieve high levels of effort and performance, and they energize people to achieve exceptional success.

A more collaborative organizational culture than the traditional one is especially important in the global, complex organizational structures required in today's multifaceted marketplace. As a consequence, many companies are evolving their overall approach toward effective teamwork and transformational leadership. Encouraging individuals at all levels to help others break through barriers and achieve common goals results in effective collaboration.

Inspiring teamwork starts at the top. A leader can empower followers by encouraging individuals to work together and demonstrating through words and actions the importance of inclusiveness and team accomplishments. Obviously, leaders who are adept at connecting people are more likely to create collaborative environments.

Increasing Organizational Performance

There is widespread agreement that being inspirational is a key leadership criterion. However, according to *The HOW Report*, published in

2011 by the advisory services firm LRN Corporation, only 4 percent of an organization's leaders actually inspire their employees.[4] This is meaningful data, given the opportunity for significant financial rewards and improved company performance in organizations with inspired employees.

The results of McKinsey's "Organizational Performance Profile" survey, conducted in 2007, demonstrated that having engaged employees translates directly into positive financial results. The proprietary survey, involving more than 115,000 individuals in 231 organizations, examined nine attributes, or "outcomes," of organizational effectiveness, and the behaviors or practices that contribute to these outcomes. A company that measures in the top, rather than the bottom, quartile of organizational performance is more than twice as likely to attain above-average margins for its industry.[5] The companies that excelled were those that actively practiced transformational leadership, known to nurture employee engagement.

Inspiring leaders build engaged and productive organizations. They also actively prioritize and invest in leader and team development. Many leaders believe they can work on their weaknesses and become better leaders, but most seem to believe that being "inspirational" is an innate quality. In reality, any leader can become more inspirational by dialing up their Grace leadership attributes: understanding and focusing on employee relationships and engagement.

Becoming an Inspiring Leader

Some researchers believe there are formulas that leaders can employ to inspire teams to achieve high levels of effort and performance, and energize people to achieve exceptional success. In an article in *Talent Management*, David C. Forman, chief learning officer for Human Capital Institute, and Friso van der Oord, the global head of research for Corporate Executive Board, outlined a set of principles of inspirational leadership that interact and build on each other.[6]

Forman and Oord claim that a leader who is trusted and collaborates across the enterprise has more impact than a leader doing just one or the other. They defined a set of six principles (described below) that characterizes inspirational leaders and emphasized how these can "leverage, propel, and inspire the organization to greater heights in a world that demands new approaches to leadership and more responsible and ethical organizations."

Rethinking and Reframing the Big Picture

Inspiring leaders know that continually rethinking and reframing the big picture is important. Decades ago, the priority in business was to keep the assembly lines operating at all cost. Any disruption in the machine approach to management was considered detrimental to the entire organization.

This is the root of the command-and-control work environment, which is suitable for the Industrial Age but not now, in what is often been referred to as the "Participation Age." Today's employees have technology at their fingertips and high expectations around authenticity, transparency, and relationships. Companies used to get away with one-way communications, with customers and employees. Today, in the participation economy, leaders must constantly innovate to keep their businesses competitive. This means nurturing a culture that enthusiastically embraces change.

One of my favorite ways to inspire employees to embrace change at Performics was to emphasize becoming comfortable as shape-shifters. I needed to imbue my teams with the confidence to constantly reframe, rethink, and outmaneuver the competition. The goal was to make sure they understood the importance of flexibility and change, and to help them to understand their role in that process.

At Performics, we provided several different iterations of our services, under very different circumstances. We provided direct services to clients where teams had direct accountability with our customers. We also provided the same services for our agency partners utilizing their brand names for their clients. In these cases, we were often silent and unseen partners, without direct client access, and the goal was to make another company look good. In yet another situation, we might be working with multiple technology partners to solve a client's need.

As a small company with client services teams trying to fill various roles, this was truly challenging and required individuals to toggle between different skill sets. This agile approach we took to solving customer problems was what I called "shape-shifting." Many of my employees thought I was a secret vampire aficionado, but really the idea came from stories told to me as a child by my great-grandmother and my affection for nature and Native American storytelling.

As mentioned in chapter 2, brain-scan research has proven that female brains are highly connected across the left and right hemispheres, and connections in male brains are typically stronger between the front and back regions.[7] Men's brains tend to perform tasks predominantly on the left side, which is the logical, rational side of the brain. Women, on the other hand, use both sides of their brains because a woman's brain has a larger corpus callosum. This means women can transfer data between the right and left hemispheres faster than men.

Women actually might be better and more comfortable than men at shape-shifting. This brain research showed women performed better at bigger-picture and situational thinking, while men performed better on more specific spatial thinking (problem solving, and pattern prediction involving objects and their spatial relationships).

Finding a Deeper Meaning

Inspiring leaders know that people want to believe in what they do and to have a meaningful role. We all spend too much time at work for it to be only a paycheck. People are seeking a higher calling for work, and more and more find that work is intertwined with life. Some research on millennials indicates that they, more than those in other generations, are demanding more from work and life and that having a workplace where they feel connected to a deeper purpose is a must.

At Performics, we created an annual "Global Performance Day," where every employee in the company around the globe participated in a full day of community service. Performics has offices in more than thirty countries around the world, and each office was empowered to choose the form of public service most relevant to its individual community. The Global Performance Day was not only significant for employee satisfaction but was also a valuable recruitment tool.

Young employees made a point to tell me they had joined the company because, unlike their previous employers, Performics had actually acted on their proclaimed company value of giving back to the community, rather than just paying lip service to the idea. They saw a demonstrated commitment to that deeper meaning. Inspiration, like confidence, is about action. In the case of millennials, that means immediate action or they respond with their own course of action.

Having a core belief and values is more than just about giving back. Believing in the culture and mission of the organization and embracing meaningful values generates self-guidance, and responsibility, as a peer, for keeping employees aligned to the organization's core set of principles and even to achieving impactful business goals.

Performics' culture was bruised when I first joined the company. It had endured three mergers in less than four years. While many members of the leadership team had prevailed through all the changes, the organization's soul had certainly taken a hit. Leadership wasn't trusted, and the leadership team felt removed from the organization. My followers didn't know me, and therefore I had to earn their trust.

Grace tends to naturally understand that culture is the organization's operating system, and that it should be intentionally shaped, developed, and enhanced. Inspiring leaders also tend to be more willing to spend time and energy focusing purely on culture. My favorite metaphor for nurturing culture is gardening. In my first book, *Marketing in the Participation Age*, I created a concept called the "Nurturist" organization: outlining a set of values for companies seeking to thrive in the Participation Age. The same concept applies here.

A leader nurturing company culture must prepare the soil and provide plenty of fertilizer and water, and a fair amount of hope and belief that it will thrive. This investment is critical, because an organization's culture is its enduring asset, significant beyond a single leader's impact; and developing a values-based culture leads to stronger business results.

Building Trust

Inspiring leaders know that trust is vital to inspiration. Trusted people are open and honest and deliver results through their actions. The conventional wisdom is that trust, like culture, just happens in a mysterious way, with little direction or control. However, most people do not realize that trust can be measured, monitored, developed, and improved.

According to the 2011 *HOW Report*, a staggeringly meager 9 percent of employees feel they work in high-trust organizations. Yet, trust is vital for employee engagement, and engagement drives company results.

Trust means leaders are open and honest with their teams, and, if a commitment is made, it must be fulfilled or an explanation is required. Trust is about leading through actions, not just words. During the first few months after joining Performics, I often stayed late working in my office. The office location at the time was less than ideal for teamwork. The overall layout was an awkward configuration, and my office was not centrally located. As a result, I couldn't really see what was happening or easily engage with others. Individuals had to make an effort to actually enter my office to see me, or I had to make an effort to see them.

After several months, a few employees began peeking around the corner into my office to say hello in the evenings, when most people had gone home. The trend seemed to gain momentum gradually, and soon a small crowd gathered each evening. I was curious to understand how they had become more comfortable and remarked about it one evening. One of the young women surprised me by saying, "Well, we saw you talking to the janitor, and so we thought it was probably okay to come in to talk to you."

Through a simple interaction of demonstrating friendliness with the janitor, I had unknowingly built trust with my team. They were watching my actions closely, and actions spoke louder than words ever could. I had built trust through my actions.

According to a survey by the U.K.'s Institute of Leadership & Management (ILM) and Management Today, "Index of Leadership Trust 2010," women CEOs were found to be more trusted than their male counterparts.[8] Women leaders had a much more intuitive response to trust and an openness to change. Women also were found to place a high value on trust, were prepared to do what it takes to build that trust, and were far more careful to ensure it isn't broken.

Trust in business translates into bottom-line results. In fact, global consulting firm Towers Watson proved that companies that developed high levels of trust were able to generate shareholder returns three times that of companies with low levels of trust.[9] Those improvements in returns are largely due to the improvement in relationships within the company—between managers and staff, between teams, and with customers and other stakeholders.

Creating a Transparent, Open Environment

Inspiring leaders know that creating a transparent environment, with open communication, is vital. Transparent means "clear enough to be seen through," according to the *Merriam-Webster Dictionary*.[10] In the workplace, the term means decisions are accessible to all; communications flow freely; people, especially leaders, are honest, direct, and clear about their motives; apologies are offered when mistakes are made; and information is shared openly with relevant stakeholders.

Information and transparency are closely related. Both are necessary for organizations to thrive in the Participation Age. As we have already discussed, infinite information is readily accessible in our world today. Followers carry around a computer in their pockets and check it numerous times an hour. Leaders and organizations must accept that universal availability of information is the norm and transparency in communication is expected, and adapt their communication policies accordingly.

Millennials, and younger generations generally, expect a transparent workplace and quickly develop a lack of trust for opaque cultures that have not evolved to this new way of working. The old Performics leadership approach that I inherited was one in which information and communication were held tightly to only the most senior leaders in the company.

When I scheduled the first all-hands meeting, I was told by my team that no one would ask questions after the presentations. It simply didn't happen at an all-hands meeting. Instead, I planted a question ahead of time with one of the team members, who asked it after the presentations. Before responding to the question, I tossed out a "prize" to this person and thanked him for asking the question. The prize came out of a box of goodies I had shopped for the day before the meeting. It was a simple, silly, yet symbolic signal that transparency was valued in the organization from the very top. After seeing the incentive, others raised their hands and never again did we hold an all-hands meeting where no questions were asked.

Transparency in leadership comes naturally to women. According to a global study, conducted by Ketchum Leadership, that polled 6,509 people across thirteen countries, participants expressed their views on effective leadership and communication, and the relationship between the two. Sixty-two percent of respondents said they believed women are better at communicating in an open and transparent way.[11]

Connecting in Meaningful and Unique Ways

Inspirational leaders know that finding a way to connect in meaningful and unique ways is essential. They establish strong bonds with their followers. This connection must be tangible, whether it is virtual or in person. One of the tangible examples of the many ways I have chosen to personally connect with followers is to hand-write thank you cards to individuals who do great work. It's a personalized touch that is unusual in a time when most of our communications are electronic.

Along with the written leadership values included in the HP Way, working at HP taught me a lot about how great leaders connect with followers. Bill Hewlett and Dave Packard created a company culture known for inclusiveness, and to be an HP employee was akin to being in a family. I will never forget, in early 2001, when I called HP CEO Lew Platt's office to inquire about securing twenty-five copies of Dave's book *The HP Way* for an agency conference I was holding in the Bay Area. Mr. Platt's assistant provided me with the number for Dave's assistant. I rang her next, and her response was classic.

"Sure, let me see if we have that many books in the garage and, if so, I will call you back," she said cheerfully.

She never asked who I was or looked me up in a directory to determine my status in the organization. I could not help but wonder whether she was going out to look in the garage for the books. Five minutes later, the phone rang again and she indicated that she found the books "in the garage" and asked if I could come "here" to get them.

I asked "where is here?" and she matter-of-factly responded, "Mr. Packard's house." I obviously agreed without hesitation, and five minutes later she faxed me the directions to the house, in the Los Altos Hills.

Upon my arrival to retrieve the books, I was greeted by Dave's housekeeper of twenty years, who gave me a tour of the beautiful residence. Along with the books, I was sent off with a bag containing four pounds of dried apricots grown on a hillside near the house.

At HP, which had eighty-five thousand employees then, I was nobody at that point. I don't believe I was even a first-level manager at the time, but, because I was an employee, I was treated like family. That experience had a deep, lasting effect on my views about company values and the importance of creating enduring, meaningful relationships with employees.

Collaborating and Participating in Decision Making

Collaboration is a means of connecting, and one form this can take is participative decision-making, engaging a group or team in the process of assessment and coming to conclusions rather than top-down pronouncements. Inspirational leaders understand this. Collaboration can take many other forms, including working together on joint projects, sharing knowledge and experience, and enabling the flow of information and talent across the organization.

Collaboration can be an especially effective leadership tool when times are tough. Consequently, women are often chosen as leaders when a company needs to change course. A research study published in 2010 by the American Psychological Association indicates many people believe men possess qualities that fit better with running successful companies, while women possess qualities that can make them a better choice in difficult situations.[12]

When asked to describe managers in successful companies, people tended to list Grit qualities that are stereotypically more masculine, such as being decisive or forceful. But when managers of companies that were struggling were asked about characteristics they desired from leadership, the number of stereotypical Grace qualities—such as being collaborative or good with people—outweighed the number of masculine ones. Often when organizations evaluate a crisis situation, they think about women leaders, perhaps because such Grace qualities are seen as particularly important to overcoming difficulties.

Some research supports the idea that women CEOs have better results in such situations. According to Susan Vinnicombe, a professor at the Cranfield University School of Management who compiles the annual *Female FTSE Board Report*, women flourished in "turnaround" situations, where a company was in urgent need of an overhaul and "required tough discipline."[13] Because of her relationship-focused style of leadership, a woman has a keen ability to tap into the spirit of individuals, even in the toughest of times.

The same is true in board situations. A study on decision making was conducted by Chris Bart, professor of strategic management at the DeGroote School of Business at McMaster University, and Gregory McQueen, a McMaster graduate and senior executive associate dean at A. T. Still University's School of Osteopathic Medicine in Arizona, and published in the *International Journal of Business Governance and Ethics*.[14] The study surveyed six hundred board directors on how they made decisions. The results indicated women are more likely to consider the rights of others and to take a collaborative approach to decision making, which translated into better performance for their companies.

I can relate to finding a collaborative turn-around situation exciting and enjoyed the challenge at Performics. As the entire organization struggled to win new business in those early days, it was critical that I showed up personally and stayed the course. This meant rolling up my sleeves, getting deeply involved in minute details, and committing to be with the team throughout the process, even if that meant staying late at night, as opposed to showing up at the last minute. These actions demonstrated my commitment to the individuals, the team, and the company—and to winning. It helped to build bridges across departments and among individuals and proved the value of collaboration. Although we didn't win at first, we stuck it out together until we did.

Inspiring Leadership: Malala Yousafzai

Several years ago at Google's Zeitgeist partner event, I was fortunate enough to be seated next to the amazingly inspirational Malala Yousafzai at lunch. Malala is Pakistani, an advocate for women's education and the youngest person ever to win the Nobel Peace Prize (in 2014). Her quiet yet determined dedication to her cause despite seemingly insurmountable challenges was simply awe inspiring. She was a teenager, yet she embodied the characteristics of someone much older and wiser. Malala's optimistic outlook was evident in her ability to see the possibilities of the future, despite the challenges she faced.

Malala's mission has been a life-threatening one for her personally: in 2012, she was shot by the Taliban and nearly died. Yet she has endured unwaveringly, deeply dedicated to her mission. Her actions have moved others and caused a tidal wave of inspiration. Malala is the embodiment of an inspirational leader. She motivates others toward greater enthusiasm and commitment to her cause by appealing to emotion and values, and by personal example.

Applying Grace and Grit to Inspire

Because the ability to inspire creates the highest levels of employee engagement and commitment, it is the quality a majority of people name when asked what they most desire in their leader. Inspiring others is very much about building relationships, thus leaders with Grace tendencies tend to have inspiring characteristics.

A leader who is trusted and collaborates across the enterprise can cause more positive change than a leader doing just one or the other. Grit tends to lead through power and status, which may be perceived as more about the leader and less about the followers. On the other hand, someone cannot obtain or maintain status without embracing power and confidence. The goal is to have a beautiful blend of both.

Historical Inspiration:
Nellie Tayloe Ross

An inspiring leader ahead of her time

Most people have no idea that the first woman in the United States to be elected governor, in 1925, was from the state of Wyoming. Perhaps that's because the circumstances were not conventional by any means.

Nellie Tayloe Ross became governor of Wyoming when she was elected to replace her husband after he died in office following appendicitis surgery. State leaders convinced her she should run as the candidate to replace him. Though she only served as governor for a short time, Nellie was an inspiring figure in politics: she was nominated for U.S. vice president in 1928 and named vice chairwoman of the Democratic National Committee that same year. She also went on to become the first woman to head a federal bureau when she was appointed director of the U.S. Mint in 1932.[15]

Nellie had few women as role models in business or politics. The scope of change that occurred for women during her lifespan is remarkable. She was born in 1876, the same year Alexander Graham Bell invented the telephone and just one hundred years after the Declaration of Independence was signed, and she died in 1977, shortly after the bicentennial celebration. She was raised during the Victorian era, when women were mostly bound to their domestic duties rather than working outside of the home, and she died when Gloria Steinem and other leaders in the women's liberation movement were gaining steam and creating unprecedented opportunities for young women.

Nellie was an unconventional leader ahead of her time, practicing transformational leadership before it had even been described as a concept. She had no prior business experience or formal management training, yet she excelled as director of the Mint, despite the fact that the department faced one of the most tumultuous times in its history. She modeled her management style on her experience raising a family.

Nellie faced a series of daunting decisions during her twenty-year tenure leading the mint, including the largest facilities expansion, and a drastic increase in coin production due to the growing post-war economy. She served four terms as Mint director, finally retiring at age seventy-six in 1953. She was known for creating a collaborative environment that involved others and always considered overall business effectiveness and long-term consequences.

During the late 1940s, Nellie implemented the bureau-wide Management Improvement Program, which closely resembled programs in the Quality Circles movement, where employees and managers were encouraged to form groups to study ways to improve processes. Quality Circles would not become widely applied in corporate America as a beneficial leadership practice until the 1980s, so Nellie was a transformational leader nearly forty years ahead of her time.

Thrust into politics following her husband's death, Nellie did not view herself as the characteristic inspirational leader of her time. I doubt that, when the state leaders approached her about running for office, she thought, "I have the charisma they are seeking." I especially appreciate that her leadership philosophy was based on treating others with respect and intimacy. Despite the challenges she faced during a difficult time at the Mint, her employees felt she genuinely cared about their welfare.

Though her story is not well known, Nellie accomplished much for the state of Wyoming and for our country, while paving a path for generations of women to come. She was a perfect blend of Grace and Grit and an inspiring leader ahead of her time.

Quick Reference Guide

Inspiring

Motivating others towards greater enthusiasm and commitment, by appealing to emotion, values, and by personal example

If you bring the Grace perspective:

- Tap into your natural ability to apply transformational leadership behaviors that improve organizational performance: people development, expectations and rewards, role modeling, inspiring others to take action, and participative decision-making.

- Rethink and reframe by reminding people of the big picture.
- Bring deeper meaning to work by providing ways for employees to channel that desire. Demonstrate this through actions, not just words.
- Earn and extend trust through actions.
- Lead with a transparent, and authentic culture.
- Connect with followers in meaningful and unique ways.

If you bring the Grit perspective:

- Balance your natural ability to drive immediate results and combine this with big-picture thinking.
- Apply transformational leadership behaviors that improve organizational performance: people development, expectations and rewards, role modeling, inspiring others to take action, and participative decision-making.
- Strive to provide employees with a deeper meaning for work.
- Understand that trust is earned and actions are required to build it.
- Remember that clear communications and transparent access to decisions and information are as important as immediate action.
- Communicate and gather input, involving team members in the process; consider others' perspectives.

CHAPTER 5

Driven

I picked up my briefcase to examine the damage and sighed in frustration. Once again, the handle was beginning to tear where it was stitched to the body of the bag. My globetrotting life was, yet again, taking a toll on the lifespan of my computer bag, and I was frustrated because, after looking high and low, this particular bag was the closest I had found to a solution that was both beautiful and functional. The rational course of action would have been to discard the damaged bag and use a backpack instead.

Backpacks are durable, have protective support for the laptop, and have a highly functional set of pockets that satisfied my desire for a structured system to organize the various odds and ends that I lug around the world. The backpack solution made even more sense, considering that I had several beautiful ones branded with the Performics logo sitting in my closet, unused. But I was determined not to compromise. Why should I be forced to choose between an attractive case and utility? Why couldn't a bag be beautiful and functional, and why hadn't someone designed something like that with women in mind?

It was 2010, and I was in the middle of writing *Marketing in the Participation Age*. I had just invested monetarily in publishing the book.

I had been working at Performics for eight months and was settling into a groove there, confident with my progress.

Without question, the last thing I needed at that moment was another project, but I was determined to find a suitable briefcase that met my personal standards. Finding a bag with a designer brand name was not a factor: I have never been one to choose a product based solely on the brand. This was about function and efficiency, combined with a classic statement of fashion consciousness. My interim solution was to alternate between two other bags, while I ordered a replacement for the damaged bag that came close to my desired design.

However, this didn't solve the problem in my mind. Between meetings and on flights, I would mull over the "ideal" bag, until one day on a flight home I found myself creating a PowerPoint presentation for the "ideal travel-bag system." I spent the following Saturday marking up my damaged bag using a Sharpie and Post-its.

I created and redesigned pockets to accommodate easy access for a wallet, a laptop, and all other travel and work materials. Easy access also meant planning for passing through airport security quickly and easily and then placing valuables back in the exact same location, so they would not be misplaced. Added to the design of the current bag was a securing back strap that enabled the bag to sit securely on top of a roller board, so it could be pulled rather than carried. To top off the design, my "system" included a small purse, as part of the briefcase, that would slip out easily and hold a wallet and phone. With this addition, the larger laptop bag could be left at the hotel when its owner went out for the evening.

I completed my design in PowerPoint, along with the marked-up prototype, and continued a thorough search for a solution already in the marketplace. I found nothing. There were beautiful bags lacking organization or durability. There were durable solutions that lacked elegance. If my ideal bag didn't already exist, I decided the next step was to build one.

Over the next several months, I set out to learn about the handbag and luggage businesses, and I got a lesson in the incredible tenacity required for anyone seeking to produce a fashion product. A New York fashion consultant informed me that just to create a first-generation cloth prototype would likely cost $50,000. This was significantly more of an investment than I had imagined. At this point, I took a few weeks to regroup, but continued to have conversations with individuals, testing the potential marketplace demand. I was determined that, if I had a need, surely others did, too, and there must be a way to bring my dream bag to life.

The parent company of Performics is Publicis Groupe. During a meeting with a coworker from another Publicis Groupe organization, the bag came up in conversation. He mentioned that his sister was the founder of a customized handbag business in Chicago called Laudi Vidni ("individual" spelled backwards). He offered to connect me with her.

That evening, I visited her website and was intrigued by her unique model, which enabled women to choose their own leathers and designs to create unique handbags. However, not a single bag on the site even remotely resembled the design of my computer bag, which was larger. In fact, my design was more akin to luggage than the designs she offered.

It wasn't long before I found myself standing in Laura Kofoid's beautiful Laudi Vidni boutique in the Lincoln Park neighborhood, where I once again presented my concept to someone who had much more fashion-industry expertise. The ambiance in the shop was amazing. It was chic, and the leathers smelled wonderful. I was impressed by the quality of the materials. Even the hardware looked and felt elegant.

Laura was even more stylish than her boutique. She dressed like an artist, and I was inspired by her own story of determination to bring Laudi Vidni to life. Laura shared how being driven and resilient ultimately paid off. Having been turned down no fewer than forty times by different leather manufacturers, she finally found one willing to partner with her to bring to life the concept of individually customized bags.

I was pleasantly surprised at how she immediately grasped the concept of the system I had designed. And, while she acknowledged that she lacked the experience of creating something that demanded the durability of luggage, she set the project in motion immediately by suggesting a meeting with her manufacturer to discuss the possibility of producing something in the luggage category. If he agreed, then they would use my marked-up bag and presentation to create a cloth prototype, which wouldn't cost me a dime.

Several weeks later, we met again at her studio to examine the prototype. It was very exciting to see my idea take shape. That prototype meeting led to another in which more refinements were made, and then came a prototype in leather. This one was durable and finished enough in appearance to test in the real world, so Laura sent me off with it to actually use it. I was so excited. It was like seeing one of my children for the first time, and I could not wait to test it.

Following several iterations, the Laudi Vidni customizable bag, now called "Diva," was formally launched as a real product. It is available to the general public today. I use my Diva every day and am forever glad that I relentlessly pursued the project, which has benefited not only me but also other traveling women who do not want to compromise beauty for function. The bag would not have happened without persistence and my intense drive to make it happen.

Driven Leaders: Results Focused and Goal Directed

In business, being driven or focused on results has been historically a highly valued leadership skill, since it can be measured more readily in dollars and cents than skills related to managing social issues that also affect productivity and profits. Moreover, individuals are much more likely to be promoted to leadership positions because of their technical or task-driven prowess instead of their relationship skills.

This is why Grit, with his focus on task-completion, is more often found in leadership positions than Grace, with her relationship-building skill set. He is the more stereotypical driven leader. Companies often promote people who lack the social skills required to make the most of their teams and do not provide these people the training they need to thrive once promoted.

"Results focused," "goal directed," and "achievement oriented" are all ways to describe the driven leader, and some studies indicate that the most effective leaders must have a high level of self-motivation to be successful. Achieving results requires a combination of strong analytical skills and an intense motivation to move forward and solve problems. It is not enough, however, to just be individually driven; a driven leader must inspire others to take action toward specific goals.

In a *Forbes* article, "What Is Leadership?," Kevin Kruse writes, "Leadership is a process of social influence, which maximizes the efforts of others, towards the achievement of a goal."[1] A leader uses social influence to engage followers and get things done.

Focusing on Goals *and* People

A 2009 survey by researcher James Zenger found employee perceptions about what makes a "great leader" to be remarkably different from what was expected. Twelve percent of the survey's respondents considered those with strong relationship skills to be great leaders. Those with a strong focus on results were seen as great leaders by only 14 percent. When both the skills were combined, however, 72 percent of respondents believed the individual would be a great leader. As it takes the confidence of followers to lead, this is an important revelation. It also proves that combining inspirational skills with strong drive can be a powerful force in driving organizational results.

Matthew Lieberman, a professor of bio-behavioral sciences at the University of California, Los Angeles, wrote about this issue in a *Harvard Business Review* article, "Should Leaders Focus on Results, or on People?" He points to a recent study that indicates only 1 percent of leaders are rated highly in both social skills and focusing on results. One percent! "We need to create a culture that rewards using both sides of the neural seesaw," Lieberman suggests. "We may not be able to easily use them in tandem, but knowing that there is another angle to problem solving and productivity will create better balance in our leaders."[2]

Perhaps the 1 percent result can be partially attributed to the fact that there are so few women currently holding leadership positions. Because women tend to be deeply focused on relationships, they may help to fill the gap in finding leaders who excel in both results and relationships. There may be a tendency to believe Grit is more focused on results, while Grace is the master of relationships, when, in fact, the combination of Grace and Grit is the most effective approach.

Anyone looking to deliver organizational results will find social skills to be a key asset. A leader with strong social skills can leverage the analytical abilities of team members far more efficiently. Having the social intelligence to predict how team members will work together also promotes teams that produce better results. The combination of focusing on both people and goals is beneficial, because sometimes what initially appear to be task-related difficulties turn out to be interpersonal team problems in disguise. Socially skilled leaders are better at diagnosing and treating these common workplace dilemmas.

Being driven by results while simultaneously focusing on people is not easy, according to Lieberman. He believes people are even more motivated by the drive for social connection than just achieving results. In his book, *Social: Why Our Brains Are Wired to Connect*, he explains that our brains' neural networks have made it difficult for us to be simultaneously social and analytical (task oriented).

Even though thinking socially rather than analytically doesn't feel radically different, evolution built our brains with different networks for handling these two ways of thinking. This might explain why people tend to be analytical or creative, but rarely both. I'm married to a guy who has amazing analytical skills, but he's not exactly socially adept, and this is quite common.

In the frontal lobe, regions on the outer surface, closer to the skull, are responsible for analytical thinking and are highly related to IQ. In contrast, regions in the middle of the brain, where the two hemispheres touch, support social thinking. These regions enable us to piece together a person's thoughts, feelings, and goals on the basis of what we see from their actions, words, and context.[3] These two networks, Lieberman writes, function like a "neural seesaw."

Lieberman conducted numerous neuroimaging studies and found that, as one of these networks became more active, the other one got quieter. In general, engaging in one of these two kinds of thinking makes it harder to engage in the other kind, although there are some exceptions. Perhaps this is why leaders tend to focus on either people building *or* task completion, but rarely both together, or to even consider them as connected.

Focusing on Relationships *and* Results

While the transactional style of command-and-control leadership has historically been more associated with men and has been the corporate-leader norm for generations, the movement toward transformational leadership is encouraging leaders to blend a results focus with inspiration and relationship skills. It's now clear that women are achieving great success using their own Grace-oriented leadership approach to driving organizational results.

According to a study conducted by Caliper Media, women in leadership roles frequently engaged in transformational leadership–style behaviors that provided intellectually stimulating environments. This encourages employees to take ownership of company goals and provides inspirational motivation, ultimately resulting in better business results.[4] In the more traditional approach to leadership, those in the highest levels of leadership own the goals. It's now more important for lower levels of followers to take ownership of results, and female leaders accomplish this by combining a focus on people *and* results.

A research study of 7,280 leaders conducted in 2011 by Jack Zenger and Joseph Folkman examined leaders in a variety of positions—from very senior manager to individual contributor. In the study, Zenger and Folkman asked others to rate the leaders in sixteen leadership competencies, and found that women out-scored men in all but one: decision-making, which also may be the most biased leadership behavior. Two traits where women outscored men by the highest margin were taking initiative and driving for results.[5]

I find that, in organizations in which stuff gets done, women are among the most talented and respected leaders. I often see women at the second or third level from the top in an organization who are more impressive than their male peers. They tend to be better liked and respected as managers and often have a talent for combining intuitive and logical thinking more seamlessly. They're more aware of the implications of their own and others' actions, and they think more accurately about the resources needed to accomplish a given outcome. Finally, they are closely in tune with their teams and excel at tracking progress towards results. The bottom-line result is that they get things done.

A McKinsey study indicated that women who successfully rise in organizations share a set of foundational strengths that fueled their growth, including a predisposition toward a results orientation. These women have a relentless focus on performance and improving the bottom line, viewing their personal success as fundamentally linked to core business results.[6]

Driven Leadership: Wenda Harris Millard

MediaLink cofounder Wenda Harris Millard credits being "driven" as the key to her career success. Her background and experience are impressive. Wenda became president and COO of advertising powerhouse MediaLink in 2009. Before joining MediaLink, she was co-CEO and president of media for Martha Stewart Living, where she oversaw media, publishing, Internet, and broadcasting businesses.

Before Martha Stewart Living, Wenda was chief sales officer at Yahoo. At the time, Yahoo was consistently credited as the number-one sales organization in the media industry, primarily because the organization's revenue rose from $700 million to more than $6 billion in just six years.

Wenda was chief Internet officer at Ziff Davis Media and president of Ziff Davis Internet before joining Yahoo. She was also a founding member of the executive team at DoubleClick (a company that went on to merge with Performics before its acquisition by Google), senior vice president and publisher of *Family Circle* magazine, and executive vice president and group publisher of *Adweek*, *Mediaweek*, and *Brandweek* magazines. Needless to say, she has had an amazing career that spans decades—and all of it in male-dominated industries.

For Wenda, being driven was an innate quality. "I have been driven since I was born," she laughed. "I think I was known for continually saying 'I would rather do that myself' from nearly the time I could speak."

Wenda recalled that, in third grade, she single-handedly redesigned the school library. "I skipped recess and rebuilt the entire elementary library, because it was a mess," she said. She explained that she was obsessed with books at the time and, because she frequently hung out at the library, she had ideas about how it could be better and was determined to make it so. Being driven is often tied to being competitive, but not always.

"I used to set goals on how many books I would read," she said. "I wasn't athletic and grew up before Title IV, and hated gym class, but I was very academically driven. I started my first newspaper, called the *Archer Lane Scoop*, when I was nine, and so even then you could see that I was driven by a hunger to produce things."

Wenda furthered her own expectations for herself and became the editor of the newspaper and literary magazine in high school and went on to accomplish the same in college.

"Most of my career in the last 20-plus years is about startups and cleanups—*Adweek*, Yahoo, and *Family Circle* for *New York Times*," she went on to explain. "They were all cleanups, and this is great for a driven person, because I understood what I needed to. It's very gratifying to save this company or create a new successful company."

I have spoken to a number of women who found that being driven as a leader can sometimes work against women. Displaying passion about driving results or encouraging teams to meet goals can be interpreted as more of a Grit style of leadership. As a consequence, some women had been told they were acting too "aggressive." I discussed this notion with Wenda, who is a generation ahead of me, to see if she could identify with this experience.

"I was very young when I got into the business," she said. "I think being driven was perceived as kind of cute when I was young, and perhaps being just a tad over five feet tall might have contributed to that because I was less intimidating.," she explained.

She admits that the leadership in the media industry is still very dominated by men. She recalled a recent meeting she attended with the CEO of a major media holding company, his president, and another high-ranking executive—all men. She went to the meeting accompanied by another male business associate.

"I was in the room, but I wasn't really in the meeting," she said. "Each time I tried to say something, someone would cut me off. Finally, at the end of the meeting one of them said, 'Aren't you the person who knows something about that *new* media?' I guess he had read my bio before the meeting."

She recalled and noted ironically that the *new* media was in fact fifteen years old. This was the only acknowledgement she received.

I asked Wenda what would have happened at the meeting if a man from her firm had not accompanied her.

"Oh, they would have canceled it," she said, without hesitation. "Men still really like to do business with other men."

While she acknowledged this, she made it clear that she does not allow this to deter her from achieving her desired outcomes or goals. Wenda attributes her undisputed success in the media industry to her innate drive and her ability to blend results with relationships.

Women's Results-Driven Skills and Abilities

The 2013 McKinsey & Company report *Women Matter 3: Women Leaders, a Competitive Edge in and After the Crisis* found that women have high career ambitions, but corporate leadership standards need to evolve to a more transformational style for them to be successful. In the survey, men and women were asked if they had the desire to reach a top management position—such as a C-suite role—in the course of their career. Seventy-nine percent of women answered affirmatively, and 81 percent of the men had the same response, revealing that women's ambitions are in line with those of their male counterparts.

The same survey revealed that nearly 40 percent of female respondents believe that women often possess leadership and communication styles that are incompatible with the prevailing styles in the top management of their companies. Thirty percent of male respondents took the same view, that the corporate culture of their organization did not foster opportunities for women to be effective in a top-management role because of the leadership style differences.

Despite the fact that companies tend to prefer Grit leadership styles, significant evidence indicates companies are adjusting to having a broader view about the unique and beneficial leadership styles that women tend to bring to organizations—especially related to managing people.

Lawrence A. Pfaff and Associates, a Michigan-based human-resource consulting firm, did a five-year study of the management and leadership skills of men and women managers. The firm found that, when rated by their bosses, themselves, and the people who work for them, women were rated significantly higher than their male counterparts.[7]

These differences extended well beyond what the study character-ized as the "softer" Grace skills, such as communication, feedback, and empowerment to such areas as "driven skills," such as decisiveness, plan-ning, and setting standards—all Grit leadership skills. The research-ers were motivated by the fact that few before them had examined the extent to which men and women leaders perceive themselves, and are perceived by colleagues—as using relational and results-oriented leader-ship behaviors in the workplace.

The goal of the study was to determine whether women leaders are perceived to demonstrate both relational and results-driven leadership behaviors by themselves, and with employees, peers, and supervisors. It also sought to demonstrate whether this critical set of leadership behav-iors is exhibited by women as frequently as by their male counterparts. Clearly, the results showed that female leaders are just as driven, if not more so, than male leaders. The real barrier for women is not their lack of ability to drive results but about organizational readiness for a differ-ent leadership style.

In another study, researchers employed the 360-degree feedback method to assess the gender differences in self-perceptions as well as the observations of the direct supervisors, immediate employees, and peers of 2,267 men and women leaders from 204 organizations scattered throughout the United States. Because women are more encouraged than men to develop their relational skills, researchers hypothesized that female leaders would perceive themselves, and be perceived by others, as employing relational leadership behaviors significantly more than male leaders, and that men and women leaders' use of more driven or results-oriented behaviors would be perceived as equal.

In this study, relational leadership behaviors were characterized as encouraging teamwork, empowering employees, coaching employees, facilitating change, encouraging employee participation, attributing rec-ognition to employees, demonstrating approachability, communicating verbally with employees, promoting trust, and delegating specific tasks.

Driven, results-oriented leadership behaviors were characterized in the study as technical expertise, directiveness, strategizing, self-confidence, decisiveness, goal setting, planning and organizing, setting performance standards, evaluating employees, and resourcefulness.

The study found that women self-reported as using their relational leadership behaviors more than men, and their task-oriented leadership behaviors as much as men. Supervisors, peers, and direct reports confirmed this self-assessment, rating women higher than men on their relational leadership behaviors and equal to their male counterparts on task-oriented behaviors.

Contrary to researcher expectations, women's self-ratings were significantly higher than men's self-ratings on five dimensions: setting goals, planning and organizing, setting performance standards, evaluating employees, and being resourceful.

Direct supervisors rated women leaders higher on communicating verbally with employees, coaching, and being approachable. There were no significant differences in ratings on teamwork, empowering employees, trust, facilitating change, delegation, participation, and recognition. Supervisors did rate women significantly higher for employee evaluation and rated men significantly higher for directiveness.

Women's Multidimensional Leadership

In same study conducted by Dr. Larry Pfaff, organizations consistently report an interest in hiring leaders skilled in employing both relational and results-focused leadership behaviors. The purpose of this study was to determine whether the small percentage of women in top leadership positions might be due to a shortage of promotable women middle managers possessing both sets of behaviors. The data analysis demonstrated that women leaders evaluated themselves and were perceived by their immediate supervisors, direct employees, and peers as excelling, even more than their male counterparts, at both the results-oriented skill set and the relational skill set. All of this research firmly validates that lack of competency or belief in lack of competency are not what is holding women back from achieving leadership roles.

When asked to describe their "ideal" leader, many employees have expressed a preference for individuals who employ both relational and task-oriented behaviors.[8] There's no question that organizations increasingly believe these multidimensional leaders may help improve organizational culture, which affects worker satisfaction and organizational loyalty. This research is noteworthy because it demonstrated that middle-management women employ both desired sets of leadership behaviors, and there should be, unquestionably, a positive effect on organizations that promote or hire women leaders.

The Danger of "Leaning In"

Clearly women possess the results-focused leadership skills needed to be effective. In terms of delivering organizational results, they naturally combine the Grace and Grit skills required in leaders that can deliver. Add in their superb and innate relationship skills, and women should be highly sought after for leadership positions. However, biases still persist, and women who are driven and demonstrate "lean-in" behaviors sometimes endure unpleasant experiences as a result.

My daughter, now in her mid-twenties, is about as focused on results as an individual can be. She is an athlete, and played volleyball and threw shot put and discus at the college level. I would describe her as one of the most motivated individuals I know. Gifted athletes have distinctive physical abilities, but their intrinsic results-driven desire is the magic that makes them superior to other individuals possessing similar physical attributes. Mesa's volleyball position was an outside hitter, despite her five-foot-seven stature. She was significantly smaller than the women who typically held that position.

Mesa got into throwing shot put and discus at the encouragement of her friends when, in her second year of high school, she decided to take up an "off season" sport. Two weeks into the track season, she convinced her throwing coach to stay after practice to help her grasp the technique better. Shortly thereafter she was throwing well enough to be recruited to throw at the college level.

Week after week Mesa stayed after practice to improve her own personal record. Those familiar with the sport will understand that there are not many five-foot-seven, 130-pound women throwers, and so, just like in volleyball, she challenged the odds despite her physical limitations.

Fast forward to her first job interview out of college. She applied for a junior-level marketing-assistant role in a medium-sized telecommunications firm. She explained to the hiring manager that she would be interested in the position for only a year and then expected to be promoted to a role beyond the assistant level. Her first round of interviews went well, and she had a brief exchange with the company CEO on her way out the door in which she shook his hand.

The following day she received a call from the hiring manager, who told her that she was exactly what they were seeking for the role, but that she needed to return to have a meeting with the CEO. She found this peculiar, because the role she had applied for had no direct interaction with the most senior leaders in the organization.

The meeting with the CEO turned out not to be an affirmation of her qualifications and fit for the role but rather a reprisal for the confidence she had exuded in her short exchange on her way out the door. He was clearly uncomfortable with her confident demeanor and ambitious aspirations. During the meeting, he asked her disheartening questions, such as: "Were you raised with humility?" and he lectured her about "leaning in," telling her directly that she had no right to aspire to a more senior role after spending a just year at the company.

I am proud to say she held herself together during the meeting, despite the fact that he gave her few opportunities to respond to his lecture and ended the meeting by asking her if she had any further questions, quickly followed by an admonition that it would be her only opportunity to respond, because she would "not see him again after today."

You can imagine how I felt when, in tears, she called me after the meeting. I resisted the urge to call and arrange a meeting with the CEO myself. I explained to Mesa that this jerk had done her a favor in the long run. If this indicated the company environment, she not would find it rewarding to work there. I have thought a lot about this incident while writing this book. I recognize that there are individuals who work in environments such as this and, without good alternative choices, may be required to simply survive in these circumstances.

I would not change who my daughter is as a person. I love that she is confident, powerful, decisive, and driven, and it is my hope that *Grace Meets Grit* will inspire individuals to embrace their own strengths. Yet

I recognize that, unfortunately, environments like this still exist in the workplace today—environments where a driven woman will be reprimanded for her strengths. I understand now that I could have done a better job of preparing my daughter for the biased perceptions and expectations that still exist in certain workplaces, while providing her with the tools and wherewithal to deal with such situations.

The takeaway here is that positive organizational results come from the coordinated effort of many people. Leaders who consistently obtain high levels of performance and effectiveness from their organizations identify and focus on goals and objectives that are truly important to the organization. They assume personal responsibility for organizational achievement, challenge others to do the same, and persist despite obstacles.

Delivering organizational results and social skills are a great multiplier for organizations seeking to reach their goals. A leader with strong relationship skills can leverage the results-driven abilities of followers far more efficiently than those focused on driving results alone. Having the social intelligence that inspires followers has proven to significantly improve results. In addition to having strong relationship skills, women possess the results-focused, driven leadership skills required to deliver outstanding organizational results.

Historical Inspiration:
The Driven Women of Jackson, Wyoming

The first group of women to govern an American town on their own

Every person who walks along the rustic wooden sidewalks in the town of Jackson, Wyoming, has the opportunity to touch a piece of history involving a group of courageous, driven women who stepped up to make a difference in 1920. With the exception of local residents, relatively few people know the story about these amazing Wyoming women from a notorious and remote town called Jackson Hole.

It all began in the spring of 1920, when concerned men and women of Jackson met for a special town meeting to discuss the numerous problems facing their tiny city. An endless stream of mud covered the streets during the spring runoff, because streets lacked drains and culverts. In addition to the mud, trash was often dumped in empty lots around town because the city didn't have a designated refuse site. And the crude road to the cemetery caused concern because getting to the hillside location by wagon could be tough. All of these issues were affecting the quality of life for town citizens, and so a group of women took it upon themselves to present to the council a formal list of grievances.

During the meeting, the mayor and councilmen seemed disinterested in any city improvements. When the discussion turned to the selection of candidates for mayor and city council, there was a general lack of enthusiasm among the men. Perhaps in jest, or out of frustration caused by the list of complaints submitted by the women in attendance, one of the men flippantly suggested, "Let's elect the women."

The evening following the meeting, a group of women gathered to form what they called the Woman's Party and, the following day, presented the citizens of Jackson with a party ticket for mayor and city council entirely composed of women. Grace Miller headed the ticket as the mayoral candidate, and Rose Crabtree, Mae Deloney, Geneviene Van Fleck, and Faustina Haight volunteered as candidates for city council. The men, many of them married to candidates on the women's ticket, moved quickly to form an opposition party and offered to the voters a slate of all men candidates for city offices.

The Woman's Party platform championed the issues they were personally passionate about and encouraged the citizens of Jackson to take action. As a result, the women won the election by an overwhelming majority. In keeping with the spirit of an all-woman city government, the council appointed only women to fill vacant administrative positions. The most colorful of these was the appointment of Pearl Williams as town marshal. The petite (five-foot tall) twenty-two-year-old woman represented herself as a tough, no-nonsense, gun-toting peacekeeper. She did carry a pearl-handled revolver, but the only outlaws she rounded up during her tenure as marshal were outlaw cattle grazing on the town square. On weekends, Pearl locked up drunken cowboys, and, if they were too much for her, she deputized her older brother to assist.

After taking office, the new mayor and city council immediately began to work on improving Jackson's infrastructure. The women quickly discovered that the treasury held only $200 and that a significant number of fines and taxes had not been collected. They set out to secure the funds owed to the city, and the money they collected increased the town coffers by $2,000, just enough to begin construction of ditches and culverts.

The beautiful raised wooden sidewalks were built with the financial aid of the parent-teacher association, and the help of the town's men. The men not only cut logs and transported them to the sawmill but also furnished the nails and the muscle to assemble a walkway from the town square to the schoolhouse. The women fulfilled their campaign promises by passing health laws that made it a misdemeanor to dump garbage in vacant city lots, establishing a refuse facility outside of the town, and constructing a road to the cemetery that would accommodate wagon and automobile travel.

Today, Jackson is known for its ski resorts and dude ranches, and for the grand views of the Teton Mountains and the direct route it offers to Yellowstone National Park. Thousands of tourists visit Jackson Hole every year, where they walk around the quaint town square bordered by elk-antler arches. As visitors walk along the raised wooden sidewalks that symbolize to tourists the true character of a Western town, most are unaware of the ambitious women of Jackson who were responsible for building the sidewalks and who made the town a better place to live nearly one hundred years ago.

Quick Reference Guide

Driven

The ability to combine strong analytical skills with an intense motivation to move forward and solve problems

If you bring the Grace perspective:

- **Leverage your relationship strengths to motivate people to take action and inspire them to go to new heights.**

- Set clear expectations and rewards for the achievement.
- Engage individuals in the decision-making process, which will inspire action on their part.
- Remember to correct course, even at the individual level, along the way.
- Remember that combining inspiration and a drive for results delivers better organizational outcomes.

If you bring the Grit perspective:

- Leverage your strengths in intellectual stimulation, efficient communication, and corrective action to keep things on track.
- Don't become so focused on the immediate outcome that you forget to build relationships and inspire people individually.
- Build participative decision-making processes, even if it takes more time and effort.
- Remember that balancing goal orientation with relationships is key to effective leadership.

CHAPTER 6

Decisive

I was walking through Zenith Media's global headquarters in New York City with a colleague who worked for another company within Publicis Groupe. I had recently moved into my role as CEO of Performics and was making a point to spend more informal time with peers, given that most of them were men and I had noticed the collegial strength of their relationships. Their informal interactions clearly indicated they were quite comfortable working together. I rarely engaged informally with them—but then, I was seldom invited. Yet, I knew I had to make a point to create informal interactions, because it was unlikely interactions would happen at all if I didn't.

Women leaders were then, and still are today, a minority in the Publicis Groupe, though this is not unique in the media holding company world. In the advertising industry as a whole, women hold just 3 percent of the leadership positions at the director level and above, despite increased visibility around diversity. As a woman CEO, I also made an effort to support other women in the company, especially those holding rare leadership positions. Rising through the ranks can be lonely, and I often found women were unlikely to prioritize time for networking at all, let alone with other women. However, carving out the time to establish relationships with other women has proven positive for me in my own career.

While working at Publicis Groupe, I also made a point to check in with senior leaders about their female direct reports. I often found that women did not receive the direct feedback from their managers that would enable them to improve their own performance.

I seized this moment with my male colleague to inquire about one of the more talented young women leaders who reported directly to him. He paused for a few minutes, seemingly surprised about the inquiry, and then shook his head, warning me the update about Kim (not her real name) was not going to be good.

"I don't think Kim is going to work out," he said.

"Really?" I exclaimed, clearly surprised and deeply disappointed, because I considered Kim to be competent and smart, with exceptional digital industry understanding and experience. It was rare to find a leader who had all of these skills within the company. She had good rapport with both her team and her clients and was always asking for feedback in order to improve. So, the news that she wasn't measuring up was surprising and upsetting.

"She can't seem to make decisions by herself," he went on, seemingly frustrated. "She's always bringing problems for me to solve. Her team is really strong, though, and most of her ideas come from them anyway."

He seemed to be making excuses about why it was better for him and the company to let her go. He went on to explain that he and Kim had already agreed upon a departure date from the Groupe, and that the separation was better for all involved.

I was shocked that the decision had already been made and that her departure date was imminent. It had all happened so quickly and without my knowledge. I had been under the impression that Kim was thriving in her role. But my knowledge of Kim was several months old and had come from information gleaned from Kim's previous boss, who had been another woman. Clearly the situation had changed when her former manager left the Groupe and Kim's reporting status had subsequently changed.

I did not recognize that this situation hinged on a gender misunderstanding associated with the decision-making leadership behavior until several years later, when one of my own direct reports at Performics brought an eerily similar circumstance to my attention. It might not have struck a chord with me even then had his words describing the "problem" not been nearly identical to the earlier conversation concerning Kim.

The male manager described the situation with his current direct report: "She is always bringing me her problems that she can't seem to solve herself." In addition, he expressed concern that this individual was taking excessive time and unnecessary effort to involve others in her decision-making process, instead of taking immediate action to solve it on her own. This behavior had caused him to question her overall leadership abilities, with decisiveness being a critical one.

This time, however, I was in a position and had the opportunity to intervene, avoiding a repeat outcome of the Kim incident. First, I asked this concerned leader if he had considered that this woman's decision-making process might have a completely different style than his own. He shook his head in response. This was obviously something he had never thought about. I then asked permission to have a conversation with the young woman in question. He agreed, and I set up a meeting.

During the conversation, it was clear that this was a complete misunderstanding based on different leadership styles. From the woman's perspective, the actions she had chosen were quite deliberate and thoughtful in approaching the decision-making situation. She, in fact, already had a solution in mind. However, she felt strongly that she had an obligation to ensure the voices of her direct reports were heard.

The woman also felt it was critical to provide her manager with an opportunity to weigh in on the decision. His opinion and voice, in her mind, were equally important to those of her followers. She had no intention of deferring the problem to her boss for him to solve for her. However, she acknowledged that she had not made that clear during her conversation with him. She was seeking his input as a sounding board before implementing a solution and also wanted him to participate in the process.

When I explained how he had interpreted the situation, she was shocked.

"Of course I involved others in the process, like any good manager would," she explained. And she seemed particularly distraught about his assessment after she approached him to consult on the situation, exclaiming, "Who else would I go to if not him? Isn't that his job?" This opened my eyes to how drastically far apart each were in their perspectives and how significant the consequences could have been without my intervention.

Women's Inclusive Approach to Making Decisions

This young woman's decision-making process exhibited a style that was consistent with all of our earlier observations about a Grace approach to leadership. She was very focused on relationships. Her goal in the process was to ensure she maintained a positive connection with her team. She sincerely felt she had an obligation to ensure their voices were heard and acknowledged, even knowing that this approach meant that additional time was required to make the decision. Thoroughness, in her mind, was most definitely valued over speed in solving the problem. She also expressed dismay that others in her shoes might skip this step altogether and move to action too quickly, as this would be, in her view, irresponsible.

All the while, her boss felt she was moving too slowly, not making progress toward a tangible end result, and involving too many others because she was not competent to solve the problem herself. He did not value others' input at the expense of losing time toward reaching a solution. He also did not understand what role she was asking him to play in her process when she asked for his input on the situation.

Unfortunately, as both examples illustrate, the consequences can be serious when Grace-versus-Grit misunderstandings occur, because being decisive is considered an essential skill for individuals at all levels, particularly for leaders.

The Most Biased Leadership Behavior

A study conducted jointly by Catalyst and the University of Michigan examined the "taking charge" leadership behaviors—namely, identifying, analyzing, and acting decisively. These "taking charge" behaviors are an area where women leaders may be particularly vulnerable to stereotype bias.[1] The study revealed that others perceive problem solving to be the aspect of leadership in which women leaders fell short of men the most, even though the research on actual leadership behavior suggests they do not. This is obviously disturbing, as men's perceptions are most likely to have the greatest effect in determining a woman's career advancement and the male style of leadership is the standard to which women are being held.

A more recent Pew Research Center study indicated this perception might be shifting a bit. Its research found the majority of individuals perceived no difference between men and women on decisiveness and ambition. However, 27 percent of adults still said that men are more decisive than women, while only 9 percent saw women as more decisive than men.[2] This, again, shows that, culturally, most people are still more comfortable with the male leadership approach to decision making.

Using Decision Making to Evaluate Leadership Performance

The fact that decision making is used to evaluate leadership performance is unfortunate, given that decision making, problem solving, and executing with excellence are considered to be the three core competencies among the essential criteria used to evaluate leadership performance. They are probably the most important key leadership performance criteria in conducting evaluations.

The Center for Talent Innovation (CTI) found that 70 percent of leaders consider decision making to be a component of executive presence for both men and women, second only to demonstrating confidence in a crisis. Clearly, decisiveness is a core aspect of gravitas and leadership effectiveness.

CTI found that being able to make decisions isn't so much the issue as needing to demonstrate decisiveness—the difference between doing the job of a leader and looking like one as you're doing it. This is why understanding that men and women approach the decision-making process differently is even more important.

As already established, the way in which women approach decision making reflects their inclusive approach to communications and to building and maintaining relationships. Similar to other leadership behaviors, Grace's approach to solving a problem or making a decision includes strongly considering the needs and wants of others. Grit, who values quick action and independence, perceives this approach as indecisiveness, with an accompanying lack of personal confidence and competence. These leadership style differences are reinforced by physiological and hormonal differences between men and women.

Biology's Influence in Decision Making

Biological differences between men and women can influence the decision-making process. As we have already established, men's brains are built for taking immediate action, both in how their brains are wired directly from front to back and are reinforced by chemical-response activities that trigger a predisposition for immediate action. Biological evidence supports the idea that men prefer to make decisions independently, as opposed to involving others in the process.

Research has confirmed that men, unlike women, become more self-focused in stressful situations.[3] The study, published in *Science Direct*, hypothesized that all people, male and female, would become more self-centered when in high-stress situations. Their rational was that becoming more autonomous and self-sufficient under stress is practical, from a biological point of view.

This hypothesis turned out to be only partially true. Surprisingly, the researchers found that stressed women actually showed higher self–other distinctions, meaning they were able to judge the emotions of other people in a way that was less influenced by their own emotional state. They were therefore able to overcome their own personal needs during a stressful situation. They also found that, for women, the act of connecting with others actually decreased their own stress. In contrast, men exposed to acute stress became more self-absorbed.

I have seen consistent evidence of this biological gender divide while conducting gender difference workshops in which men and women are paired together and provided with the same high-stress work scenario.

The paired individuals are asked to outline their personal approach to tackling the problem first, before sharing their strategies with their partner. In nearly every team, the men specified activities that indicated their preference for working alone first in order to focus individually on the challenge. The men also outlined problem-solving activities in which they worked independently, especially in an urgent, high-stress situation. The more urgent the situation, the more men limited the involvement of others. On the other hand, women consistently indicated their preference to immediately seek out others and work collectively by asking questions and building consensus as a strategy for solving the problem.

Physiology's Reinforcement of Decisive Behaviors

The differences described above could be attributed to other physiological differences. Because of their cognitive strengths, men often attack problems by isolating components and optimizing point solutions, whereas the female brain's integrative advantage can lead women toward maximizing solutions that aim for greater, more holistic outcomes. Furthermore, the *Science Direct* study indicated that women might, in fact, handle stress better, because they release higher oxytocin levels under stress. Oxytocin has been shown to improve mind reading,[4] enhance emotional empathy,[5] and sharpen self-other perception.[6] This might also explain why men react differently under stressful conditions.

Other factors shed light on what drives the behavioral differences. According to a 2005 study conducted at the University of California, Irvine, men's brains have approximately six-and-one-half times more gray matter than women's, and women's brains have nearly ten times more white matter than men's.[7] Because gray matter characterizes information processing centers and white matter facilitates the connections among those centers, scientists theorize that these differences might explain why men tend to excel in tasks that depend on sheer processing, while women show relative strength in tasks that call for assimilating and integrating disparate pieces of information. It also indicates that not only are women more predisposed to gather information but they also process it more easily after collection.

This would seem to suggest that, if a man were to take a woman's approach to decision making, requiring him to assimilate information from a number of sources, the process itself would be more difficult for him, not just unfamiliar, and vice versa.

All of this research reinforces the notion that behavioral dissimilarities will persist because of the biological distinctiveness of men and women. Understanding the consequences of these differences as they relate to specific leadership behaviors expected in the workplace has implications for both individual and organizational effectiveness. But the impact goes beyond man-woman misunderstandings between individuals or solving specific workplace disagreements.

Decision-Making Differences and Sales Processes

As more women become decision makers in corporate settings, companies have recognized that a change in their sales process is required for them to win business from companies in which women are making the choices. After several unsuccessful business pitches in which women were prevalent decision makers on the other side, Deloitte conducted research around this very issue and published some of the outcomes in an article in *Harvard Business Review*.[8]

The Deloitte study found that, during a sales process, women perceive an important meeting with a potential service provider as a chance to explore options in collaboration with an expert resource. Men, on the other hand, see that event as a near-final step in the process, when they are narrowing down and choosing among options.

Another noted difference is that traditional male purchasers want the buyer's power over the seller to be acknowledged. This behavior is consistent with the male decision-making approach, where power and authority are actively considered as an integral part of the process. Because traditional sales processes have been geared more toward the Grit perspective, high-ranking people from the seller organization often have a practice of appearing at meetings to signal the importance of the project. Access to a high-ranking company executive is an action that plays to those influenced by power and status.

The sales team at Performics often requested my presence as CEO at a hosted dinner following a pitch by the team. The team assumed my presence would clearly demonstrate the importance of the client's business to Performics and that inviting prospective customers to an exclusive, intimate dinner with the CEO made an impact. This strategy works well if the customer is status conscious. But, if the team accountable for the decision are predominantly women, this custom might not be effective at all.

Women's View of Status Rituals

Deloitte's research found that women were less likely to see the value of status rituals. In a woman's mind, high-ranking individuals were welcome to join the discussion—but for their experience and insight, not their position. The study found that it was more important to women buyers to meet the people they would be working with day-to-day, rather than meeting management. As would be expected, the women were much more focused on building the relationship with potential partners than having dinner with someone they might never see again and who did not provide lasting value to them personally or their organization.

Women's predisposition to favor relationships was also revealed when Deloitte proposed a large advisory project to a big technology company. The client audience was mixed: three women and two men. The prospective client insisted that only three people from Deloitte be present at the meeting. Consequently, Deloitte chose not to include the highest-ranking leader, and instead flew in a manager from India, where the majority of the work they were bidding to do would occur. This turned out to be a good decision. The client later told Deloitte that having the Indian manager present in the meeting was critically important and that it was essential for the client to meet her counterpart on the Deloitte team. This is another excellent example where women valued the relationship over status.

Finally, Deloitte noted that women valued the scope of consideration beyond simply solving the immediate business problem and, moreover, viewed it as an opportunity to consider a larger business outcome. A woman decision-maker was interested in understanding the broader benefits of partnering not just for her company but also for the members of the team she was responsible for developing. Conversely, men decision-makers were much more focused on the immediate and shorter-term business needs.

Similar behavior has been found in more-senior organizational leaders, such as corporate directors. A 2013 study of more than 600 corporate board directors published in the *International Journal of Business Governance and Ethics* found that women directors were more likely to consider the rights and opinions of others and feel it was important to take a more cooperative approach to decision making in order to arrive at a fair and moral decision that benefited all parties.[9] They also engaged in more collaboration and consensus building, not only in an attempt to make sound decisions but also to garner support for a course of action. The study's authors also observed that women directors engage more effectively with the complex social issues and concerns that increasingly confront corporations.

It's clear that men and women have different perspectives and processes when it comes to decision-making behaviors in the workplace, and these differences are not likely to change any time soon given, the reinforcing physiological differences between the sexes.

Decision Making Combining Grace and Grit

From a broader perspective, having organizational leaders who are able to view situations objectively and rationally and proactively collaborate with others can be very beneficial for the organization at large. This emotional-intelligence approach to decision making is consistent with transformational leadership. Emotional intelligence has been proven to enhance leaders' ability to solve problems and to address issues and opportunities facing them and the larger organization.

Transformational leaders have been found to apply a more inclusive, rational approach to decision making. This is because they are able to separate their own emotions more effectively from the situation. They are also able to determine whether the emotions are linked to opportunities or problems and use those emotions in the process of decision making.[10] It has already been established that women apply transformational behaviors more often than men. While these are obviously more positive for the organization, they may not be recognized in the heat of the moment, when men, who are more often than not the more senior leaders, are evaluating a woman's behaviors against how they would approach the situation.

In facing a critical business decision as a CEO, I wanted people with diverse perspectives sitting at the leadership table to understand all aspects of the decision. Having individuals who are hungry to immediately attack the situation and solve the problem in an urgent fashion, as the more traditional Grit perspective would provide, is a critical skill set. But having individuals who are able to more easily separate themselves from the situation and include the broader organization in forming a solution, as the Grace perspective brings, are invaluable as well. Both Grace and Grit demonstrate decisiveness in their own way.

Until we challenge the status quo approach to the corporate leadership style and get more women executives seated at the table, each comfortable with bringing her individual approach to leadership, organizations will miss out on the opportunity to leverage the decision-making power that having both the Grit and Grace perspectives provides.

Historical Inspiration: Esther Hobart Morris

A justice of the peace must be decisive

Esther Hobart Morris was a brave, tough pioneer woman. Even by the standards of pioneers who had a well-known physical and mental fortitude for survival, her little-known story is compelling. She was the first woman to become justice of the peace in the United States, appointed in South Pass City, Wyoming, in 1870.

Colorful stories and historical accounts about Esther abound. She was a leader in the passage of Wyoming's suffrage amendment before being named justice of the peace. According to historical society reports, she once jailed her own husband after he reportedly made a scene in her courtroom. This must have been a bit awkward, given that court was held in her log cabin, where Esther reportedly sat on a wood slab in the living room. She ruled on twenty-seven cases during her more than eight months in office.

Ironically, the Sweetwater County Board of County Commissioners appointed Esther to the seat after the previous justice resigned in protest of Wyoming Territory's passage of the women's suffrage amendment. Wyoming became the first jurisdiction in the United States to grant women the right to vote when the territorial governor, John A. Campbell, approved the constitution in December 1869.

Staying true to the territory's vigorous support for equal rights, the county clerk telegraphed a press release announcing the historic event of the first woman justice of the peace. The clerk's telegraph to the world in part read as follows:

"Wyoming, the youngest and one of the richest territories in the United States, gave equal rights to women in actions as well as words."

Like most residents of the time, Esther was not a native to the wilds of Wyoming. Born in New York and orphaned at an early age, she apprenticed to a seamstress and ran a successful millinery business out of her grandparents' home. Even at an early age, she was reported to be decisive in her opposition toward slavery, countering efforts of slavery advocates who threatened to destroy a church that supported abolition.

After her first husband's death, she moved to Illinois, where she later married John Morris, becoming Esther Morris. In 1868 they relocated to South Pass City to open a saloon. This was a difficult journey for a woman of her age; she was fifty-five years old at the time. She first traveled by train to a waystation on the newly completed Transcontinental Railroad at Point of Rocks, twenty-five miles east of present-day Rock Springs. From there, Esther Morris and her family continued north by stagecoach, ascending a gradual mountain pass to a mining district.

The stark, dry, rocky landscape that confronted Esther as she stepped off the stage coach at South Pass City must have appeared startlingly different from the tame landscapes she had known in Illinois and New York. She and her husband constructed their new home, which involved constructing a twenty-four-foot by twenty-six-foot log cabin with a sod roof, in a barren gulch at the mouth of a canyon near the Continental Divide, 7,500 feet up in the Rocky Mountains.

The Morrises were one of the few families who lived in this remote mountain village year-round. Winters must have been brutal for them, residing as they were at a high elevation in a primitive cabin. Most South Pass residents either left the area for the long winters or faced extreme hardship and isolation during them. Those who stayed battled sub-zero temperatures, high winds, and deep snow that might not retreat until June.

Esther Morris is yet another example of an extraordinary Wyoming woman who possessed a leadership style where Grace meets Grit. She exemplified the pioneer spirit in many ways and defied the odds to make her a community a better place to live. Though she lacked any prior experience or training as a justice of the peace, she worked diligently to rule on each decision brought before her in a timely manner, acted in the best interests for all parties involved, and used the resources that she had at the time.

Quick Reference Guide

Decisive

The ability to make decisions in a timely and effective manner, resulting in a desired outcome

If you bring the Grace perspective:

- Demonstrate immediate action as an incremental step to gathering information. If you are reporting to someone with the Grit perspective, a helpful tip to demonstrate your focus on immediate outcomes might be to summarize your actions ahead of a meeting or as a follow-up, to signal that speed is a priority.
- If you choose to use your boss as a sounding board, and he has the Grit perspective, clarify the role you are asking him to take in the process.

- Sorting solutions into short-term and long-term approaches can be helpful in remembering both are important.
- When presenting solutions to a group with primarily a Grit perspective, focus on the immediate actions first. This will help them avoid missing the longer-term opportunities.
- Don't forget power and authority, especially with peers. Balance getting a fresh perspective with communicating your opinion.
- Maintain an inclusive, empathetic, and relationship-focused team approach to solving problems. Thorough communications, involve the team in the process, and follow through with actions.
- Despite the pressure to abandon your own tendencies to capably separate your own needs and emotions from the situation, stay true to Grace and leverage your inclusive and relationship power, as it is beneficial to the situation and the organization.

If you bring the Grit perspective:

- Don't forget that communicating to the team and involving others in the process is just as important as immediate action.
- Demonstrating immediate action and urgency is valuable to the situation, so bring your strength.
- Sorting solutions into a short-term and long-term approach can helpful in remembering both are important.
- Don't forget the value of the bigger picture, even though there is urgency in the moment.
- Maintain an empathetic and relationship-focused team approach. Thorough communications, involve your team in the process, and follow through with actions. If you are confused about the role you are being asked to play by someone with the Grace perspective, ask.

CHAPTER 7

Confident

My father spent much of his life working on big cattle ranches as head foreman. This meant that, for most of my childhood, I lived in remote communities in Eastern Oregon. "Community" might even be an exaggerated term, because the towns where we resided were so tiny and remote that populations were often fewer than one hundred souls.

The middle of nowhere in the West was a wonderful place to grow up, and this is probably why I still call it home today. I also found the lessons I learned growing up on a ranch valuable to my later work life. I developed, among other things, an acute awareness of my surroundings and the interconnectedness of all things. I learned how to be content with silence and hunger for independence. I fell in love with horses and still own one and continue to ride today.

By the time I was enrolled in middle school, I had acquired sufficient equestrian skills and confidence to ride my horse for miles each day during the summer, unaccompanied by an adult. My friend, who lived across the gravel street from my house, and I would leave our homes very early in the morning, sometimes before dawn, and pick a direction to ride for the day. Our parents had no idea what route we had chosen. Sometimes we would not return home until late in the afternoon. We explored canyons and caves, raced across the high desert at breakneck speed—sometimes without saddles—embracing the joy of our youth with open, free hearts.

Looking back, I think about our courageous pursuit to ride better, longer, and further and to explore anything and everything we encountered, embracing the adventures each day would bring. It was pretty obvious that we never thought about our appearance. Looking back at old photographs, I see a girl who looked and dressed more like a boy, wearing pants and shirts of unmatched plaid. Instead, our time and energy were spent working with our horses as a team, making sure we were all headed in the same direction, and that we had a great time. These are still things I focus on with a team today.

The exhilarating connection of being one with a horse has provided me with countless lessons over the years, and I continue to learn each time I step up into the saddle. Confidence and conviction are fundamentals when riding (for both the horse and the rider), because the rider must believe the horse will do what it is asked and the horse must believe the rider has the ability to lead.

A human cannot physically force a horse to do anything it does not want to do—on the ground or in the saddle. A horse is simply too physically strong. The rider must convince the horse by her presence that it should do what she requests. This requires trust, respect, charisma, persuasion, and, above all, confidence.

Interacting with a horse and developing a relationship with a team have numerous similarities. The easy part is creating the vision and knowing where to go, and even telling the team we're headed there, while the more difficult part is earning enough confidence to persuade others to follow. Like people, every horse is a unique individual, so a good horsewoman knows her horse and adjusts her style to achieve the best results. The same is true about good leaders and followers.

Horses are social herd animals that depend on having a leader for their survival. Consequently, they do conform to a hierarchy of sorts. For their own safety, they choose to be a part of a group of horses, such as a band or a herd. Leaders in the horse world must be bold and confident in their choices, because they are accountable for making decisions that affect the safety of the entire herd, and they earn their position by demonstrating confidence.

From the moment a rider approaches a horse in the pasture or stall and removes it from the herd, she becomes the designated herd leader in the relationship. At that moment, the horse is placing its trust in the rider's hands. The connection continues literally through the reins, where the rider continually communicates with the horse, guiding and reassuring it. There are legends from Portugal that describe the oneness between horse and rider as an invisible, golden thread, where both creatures have remarkable sensitivity to one another's subtle energy shifts. This analogy is also thought to be related to the legend of the centaur, a mythological creature that has the head, arms, and torso of a human, and the body—including four legs, hindquarters, and tail—of a horse.

I have spent my entire life in pursuit of that powerful feeling of connectedness with the horse. Sometimes those moments are fleeting and last only for a few seconds. I feel the same about the pursuit of leadership. Through experiences, both those that are good and those that are more challenging, I am continually striving to develop the skills needed to be a better leader for the organization, individuals in it, the business, and me. Like the poetic metaphor of the golden thread, building and maintaining a connection with individuals and a team can be difficult to achieve, particularly if the leader lacks confidence.

Quantifying Confidence

What exactly is confidence? It is often described as a feeling or belief in someone. Because it's a feeling, as a leadership behavior it is difficult to quantify, perhaps because it is a quality that comes from within, measured by external appearance, and its assessment is subjective.

According to Georgetown University linguistics professor Deborah Tannen, the only evidence individuals have to judge confidence in another person is circumstantial and tied to specific behaviors. Mostly these behaviors are related to how someone speaks about what they know. This includes facial expressions and body posture, but, most of all, speech. Does the person speak up or stumble over their words? Is his or her tone declaratory or halting?[1] Because people judge confidence purely on appearance, the behavior can be problematic for women, in particular.

Gender Differences Regarding Certainty and Doubt

As Tannen explains in her book *Talking from 9 to 5*, women are more likely to downplay their certainty, while men are more likely to downplay their doubts. She attributes this to early cultural training, where girls learn when they are quite young that sounding sure of themselves will cause them to be unpopular with their peers. This is quite the opposite for men, who need to project confidence to establish and maintain status.

A woman's relationship-focused communication style also influences how women demonstrate confidence. The relationship focus means women tend to balance their own interests with those of the person they are addressing, taking that person's feelings into account and adjusting their own style throughout the conversation to accommodate the other person's needs. Obviously, if speech is one of the most critical considerations in how a person's confidence is gauged, this may negatively affect the perception of whether a woman possesses confidence.

Speech is not the only consideration when it comes to unlocking this complex leadership behavior. Having an ambiguous relationship with power and ambition, and focusing on competence instead of confidence, are all key limitations for women seeking to obtain and retain confidence.

Women's Focus on Competence, Not Confidence

Late in my tenure at Hewlett-Packard, I was having dinner with my husband, Rob, and talking about work in general. At that time, I was sharing my thoughts about the printing-business strategy, the industry, and what I anticipated for the future outlook of the business as a whole. One of the things I love about the person I married is that I can have this level of strategic conversation with him. He's intelligent, knowledgeable about the technology industry in general, and often serves as a great confidant, fulfilling my own need for a sounding board.

"You should run a company," he said to me during this particular conversation. "You have the mind for it. You understand strategy, can see around corners, and you're an inspirational leader."

At the time, I took his comment as an extraordinary compliment (however biased—he is my husband, after all) but didn't take it seriously. I had never really thought about becoming the leader of an entire organization. What did go through my mind were all of the skills and experience I lacked, such as an advanced degree, hands-on experience with profit and loss, etc., etc., etc. The idea of my actually attaining such a role seemed unimaginable.

Numerous times after this conversation, Rob reminded me that his opinion hadn't changed and he felt the CEO role would be "the perfect fit" for me. I honestly blew it off each and every time. During one of these self-deprecating dialogues, he pointed out that I was the one limiting my own potential by dismissing the idea as even a possibility. He had a point.

I did not fully appreciate Rob's view until after I departed HP and joined Moxie Interactive, a Publicis Groupe company, as a senior vice president. When I initially considered joining Moxie, I felt the new role was a meaty one that matched my qualifications and experience but also provided me with a robust challenge, enabling me to continue to grow.

After several months in the new role, however, I knew that I had undershot my capabilities. I had underestimated the preparation my HP experience afforded. I actually possessed many more qualifications and competencies than I realized and understood finally the complete value I could contribute for the entire business, beyond the four departments I was leading. Fortunately, the Moxie leaders allowed me to continually color outside the lines of my role, and rewarded me with a seat at the executive team table. Otherwise the position would have lacked the challenge required to keep me satisfied.

A year later I had the first conversation with my manager about the CEO position at Performics. He began the conversation with, "Too bad you don't want to run a search firm based in Chicago." I looked at him rather perplexed, because I knew exactly which search firm he was referring to and he knew I was passionate about that company. I also felt a bit slighted, because his comment implied that he already knew I wasn't interested.

I quickly responded before really thinking it through: "What do you mean, 'too bad you're not interested'?" I asked. "Are you asking me if I *am* interested in the role? I am most definitely interested."

It was an assertive, confident response. I had not demonstrated a single ounce of indecision. This turned out to be exactly the forthright conviction he was seeking.

I'm not sure why I reacted in such an outspoken manner. This was exactly the role I had told Rob I would never be interested in, nor qualified for, and as silence filled the room while I waited for my boss's response, I remember feeling both excited and terrified. Despite all my concealed doubts, that quick and confident response set me on the path to the most satisfying role in my career at the time. Looking back, I wonder what would have happened had I hesitated in my response, or told him I wanted to think about it first.

Cost of the Confidence Gap

The confidence gap between women and men is well documented. Katty Kay and Claire Shipman, authors of *The Confidence Code: The Science and Art of Self-Assurance—What Women Should Know,*[2] have conducted extensive research about the topic. The two stumbled upon confidence as a meaningful issue and potential leadership barrier for women in their first book, *Womenomics,* published in 2009. Several years later, they wrote a more comprehensive book specifically about confidence. In it, they cite numerous studies that validate the unfortunate fact that a vast confidence gap appears to separate men and women.

Kay and Shipman also found that leadership success is directly cor-related to confidence, not competence. Rising through the ranks as a successful leader and being proficient in competencies is not sufficient. This was troubling because they suspected that women were choosing to focus on competence instead.

Their research affirmed that women value competence as the key criterion in career advancement and tended to base their decisions on whether to pursue a leadership position on whether they believed they possessed *all* the competencies before they would consider applying for a role. To make matters worse, women also tended to be harsher on their own assessment of those competencies than men. Other studies have confirmed this finding. A 2011 survey conducted by ILM, for example, found that half of female managers doubted their job performance and careers, compared with less than a third of male respondents.[3]

Katty Kay and Claire Shipman found several interesting examples. For nearly a decade, professor Marilyn Davidson at the Manchester Business School, also in the U.K., has requested that her students complete a questionnaire about what they expect to earn and what they deserve to earn five years after graduation. Consistently, she has found striking differences between male and female responses. On average, she reports, the men believe they deserve $80,000 a year and women $64,000 a year—or 20 percent less.[4]

Gender Differences in Estimating Competence

To make matters more complicated, research has found that men tend to *overestimate* their competence and their performance while women tend to *underestimate* both. In every case, actual performance did not differ as it related to the quality of work output. Women, in fact, had the same or greater level of actual skills and abilities required to deliver equal results as men did, but lacked conviction in them.

Cornell psychologist David Dunning and Joyce Ehrlinger of Washington State University studied the specific correlations between confidence and competence. This research followed an earlier body of work that has come to be known as the "Dunning-Kruger effect," or the tendency for people to substantially overestimate their abilities. In fact, Dunning and Kruger have found that the *less* competent people are, the *more* they overvalue their abilities and are confident in them. This study did not take gender differences into consideration.

The Relationship of Competence to Confidence

To build on the original work and focus specifically on gender differences, Dunning and Ehrlinger gave male and female college students a quiz about scientific reasoning. Before administering the quiz, the researchers asked for individuals to rate themselves on their scientific skills. The intent was to find out if students' confidence in their science competence truly affected their actual competence.

The second example highlighted by Kay and Shipman is from Dunning and Ehrlinger who found women rated their competence more negatively than the men did, giving themselves an average of 6.5 on a scale of 1 to 10, while men gave themselves a 7.6. When it came to assessing how well they felt they had answered the questions on the quiz, the women thought they got 5.8 out of 10 questions right, while men assumed 7.1. In reality, the difference between their scores differed only slightly, with women answering 7.5 out of 10 correctly and men, 7.9.[5]

The list of studies confirming the propensity for women to under-value their own qualifications and competence is long and, honestly, depressing. I have had a number of conversations with women who doubted their own qualifications for a job opportunity and decided not to apply because of it. But these women also questioned the competence of men who, despite their similar credentials deficit, eagerly raised their hand for the same role. The women expressed frustration and even dis-dain for the fact that someone who clearly wasn't qualified would have the audacity to apply for the job. As this example illustrates, the fact that women place a higher value on competence often holds them back. Men, on the other hand, have a very different perspective.

The research that relates to how Grit values competence and confi-dence can be enlightening for Grace, who believes that men knowingly pursue opportunities that exceed their own capabilities.

Men's Tendency Toward Overconfidence

Columbia Business School professor Ernesto Reuben and his colleagues published a study in 2011 indicating that men do not consciously attempt to fool anyone into believing they are more competent than they actually are. However, men are naturally overconfident and actu-ally believe they are qualified, even if they have only a few of the creden-tials outlined in a job specification.[6]

This study also highlights the organizational effect of women's lack of confidence. The study found women are selected 33 percent less often than they should be on the basis of their actual abilities. This suggests that the underrepresentation of women in a competitive environment is not always due to overt discrimination or to gender differences in preferences but rather to the fact that men tend to be overconfident when they recall their own abilities and women are underestimating theirs.

The Columbia University study reaffirmed two earlier studies showing that the relative performance of women versus male counterparts actually worsened when they were in competitive situations, particularly when the person they were competing against was a man. Both studies found that women prefer to opt out of competitive situations altogether, even when it was financially beneficial for them to participate.[7] Men's confidence, on the other hand, was unfazed when confronted with a competitive situation. This is particularly disturbing, because, statistically speaking, most of the time women are competing against men for leadership positions. And climbing the leadership ladder is a competitive situation. Unfortunately, a woman's lack of confidence does not seem to improve with age or experience.

Another ILM study found that men are much more confident than women across all age groups. In leadership positions, the discrepancy was particularly significant, with 70 percent of male managers having high or quite high levels of self-confidence, compared with just 50 percent of women. Half of women managers admitted to having feelings of self-doubt, compared with only 31 percent of men.[8]

The Link Between Confidence and Ambition

The same study found a strong link between managers' confidence levels and ambition. Women who had low confidence exhibited much lower expectations about reaching a leadership and management role as well as about achieving their career ambitions.

The important takeaway is that Grit is more willing to put himself forward for leadership roles, even if he does not meet the full criteria for the role. The study showed that 85 percent of women would only apply for a position if they thought they met the job description "fully" or "pretty well." Confidence represents a leadership behavior where Grace and Grit tend to have vast differences, and in general, Grit tends to be overconfident while Grace tends to be underconfident.

I once interviewed my boss's wife to complete a biography about him as part of an entry for a significant industry award. I asked her what she felt inspired him to achieve greatness in his career. She said that, despite his humble beginnings and limited experience, he approached every opportunity with a simple philosophy: "Why not me?" This mind-set, accompanied by the absolute belief that he could bring value to every opportunity, had propelled him to amazing career heights, despite his competency level or lack of experience.

Physiology and Confidence Differences

Brain science may provide insight about additional factors that contribute to why men possess greater confidence. Women tend to activate the amygdalae—the two parts of the brain involved in processing emotional memory when responding to stressful situations—more often than men. This suggests that women may have a greater emotional response to negative events.

Women are also more likely to dwell on past negative experiences, because the anterior cingulate cortex—the part of the brain that helps us to recognize errors and weigh options—is larger in women. And, finally, the predominance of estrogen, which discourages conflict and risk taking, may play a role in hindering confidence in women.

In contrast, men have built-in, confidence-bolstering kryptonite in the form of the hormone testosterone, known to cultivate risk taking. Obviously, a strong appetite for taking chances has both positive and negative consequences. An overabundance of testosterone in animals has been known to cause aggression, overconfidence, and even fatal risk-taking.

How to Show Confidence

Effective leadership requires confidence and even though this behavior may not come naturally for some women, there are proven methods to display it to others. Confidence is fundamentally a mind-set choice, and the key to overcoming a lack of confidence is action. I have had many women acknowledge this and then ask, "That's great, but how do I get started?"

Five Steps to Gaining Confidence

Grace Killelea, author of *The Confidence Effect: Every Woman's Guide to the Attitude That Attracts Success*, recommends faking confidence as a first step toward building it over time. Her advice is to practice these behaviors until confidence becomes a habit of sorts.[9] Killelea, who has spent her career as a leadership coach, suggests establishing confidence using the following five steps:

1. Practice establishing a physical presence by portraying a confident body posture. Stand up tall. Sit back and take up space in a seat. Sit in a power position in the room and at the table.
2. Speak with assurance without thinking about how the idea might be shot down. Don't hesitate to speak up even if the idea isn't fully formed.
3. Stop apologizing and worrying about being liked. This is the one exception where relationship skills may actually get in the way. Don't worry about being overly collaborative, as it may also work against having a confident presence.
4. Focus on representing a factual point of view. Speak truthfully about abilities or accomplishments and be assured this is not bragging. Don't worry as much about competency.
5. Turn off the critical and negative self-talk in your head.

Taking Up Space and Speaking with Assurance

Psychologist Cameron Anderson of the University of California, Berkeley, has spent his career studying overconfidence. His studies repeatedly point to the fact that individuals who are self-assured and confident are also those most admired and listened to, regardless of the organization or situation. He believes confidence manifests itself in body language, specifically in taking up space in the room, speaking calmly and at a lower tone—and early and often—but in a relaxed manner.[10]

This combination also works beautifully to calm a rattled horse. I can't think of many situations more formidable than sitting upon a 1,200-pound animal fighting for his head and threatening to rip the reins from your hands in an effort to give in to his own innate desire to flee an uncomfortable situation. In that moment, the rider must actively engage the horse by speaking calmly and in a low tone, and blowing air out of the lungs to be able to sit back and take up space in the saddle.

For me, this metaphor has become a powerful visualization tool for regaining confidence. If I feel my confidence wavering, I imagine I am riding my horse and he's the one experiencing the confidence gap. I must take quick action to reestablish the role of a leader, taking the actions mentioned above. My internal voice can remind me that I am the confident leader. Conference room or saddle, it works in either situation.

Stimulating Action by Overbelieving

Kay and Shipman claim it is better to overbelieve in your capabilities, because this can stimulate action faster than just thinking about actions, or worrying about doing something. Not only can hesitation affect confidence, it can also have an impact on actual results. A lack of confidence leading to inaction results in a lack of productivity. This is a great example of how all of the leadership behaviors described in *Grace Meets Grit* are interconnected. A leader's inability to deliver results obviously often results in undesirable consequences that are more serious.

Taking Action

As Killelea's five steps imply, action is the key to building confidence. Ohio State University psychology professor Richard Petty has spent decades focused on the study of confidence. His definition of confidence, quoted in a *Harvard Business Review* article by Francesca Gino and Gary Pisano, is a reminder of what is required to obtain it and why taking action is critical: "Confidence is the stuff that turns thoughts into action. Action bolsters one's belief in the ability to succeed. In other words, confidence accumulates through actions. In the workplace, this can be in the form of hard work, success, and even through failures."[11]

Applying quick action sounds like an easy fix, but actually may be more difficult for Grace, because, as brain research reveals, women tend to overthink a situation and to delay any form of action, which might then reinforce the lack of confidence. Negative self-talk and paralyzing overanalysis that prevent taking action can become a vicious, reinforcing circle. For Grit, confidence is the fuel that drives action, and taking action increases his confidence. No wonder Grit tends to be overconfident and Grace, underconfident!

Displaying confidence is critical for transformational leaders. Confidence is required to establish and achieve a vision. Followers need to have confidence in their leader and his or her vision to deliver their part, and the leader needs to have confidence in the followers' capability to achieve their part. Confidence drives cohesion within the team. Unlike many of the previous leadership behaviors discussed, confidence is an area where Grace may have to work harder, because these skills might not come as naturally.

Grace can leverage the innate authentic and transparent style that is so effective for transformational leaders, but must also remember that followers are looking for cues from their leader that inspire confidence, and this is likely to be more important to followers than having deep skills and abilities. Displaying conviction about the mission might be the most important skill a transformational leader can possess.

All of these may sound easier to implement than they actually are, for all the reasons previously mentioned. A final tip that I, personally, have found most helpful is adopting a growth mind-set. Carol Dweck, in her book *Mindset: The New Psychology of Success*, encourages people to believe that all skills can be developed through hard work and commitment and that wherever you are is a good starting point.[12] This is different from assuming a more black-and-white, fixed mind-set of someone who believes there is no hope for improving the skills and abilities they currently possess.

Adopting a growth mind-set is about assuming a more empowered position that demands a call to action. As we have already learned, taking that action will in turn drive confidence.

Historical Inspiration:
Eliza Stewart Boyd

The first woman in America to serve on a jury

If women could vote, they could also serve on a jury, and Wyoming gave women the right to vote in 1869. In March 1870, Eliza Stewart Boyd's name was drawn to serve on a grand jury. Wyoming made history again a few months later when five other women from Laramie were the first women in the world to serve on a trial jury.[13]

Like nearly all of the pioneer women who accomplished firsts, Eliza Stewart moved to Wyoming after growing up in the East. She was quite educated for her time, graduating as class valedictorian from the Washington Female Seminary in Washington, Pennsylvania, when she was twenty-eight years old.

Eliza taught school in Pennsylvania for eight years before moving west to Laramie in 1868. She was not married at the time. No one knows what inspired her to travel all the way across the country to one of the wildest Western outposts by herself, without a job, but clearly it required confidence to take such a bold step. Her passion seemed to inspire her actions, and this move to the untamed West was just the first of many bold steps she took that helped shape the state's early history. The timing of her arrival was fortuitous, because the first public school was scheduled to open soon and was in need of a teacher. Eliza was hired and became the first teacher to work in the Laramie public schools.

Eliza met her husband, Stephen Boyd, in Wyoming and served on the grand jury before their wedding ceremony. Shortly after her marriage, she was named to the organizing committee for the Wyoming Literary and Library Association, which was dedicated to the promotion of libraries and arts. There she helped to draft the constitution and became a charter member of the organization. She is among the many extraordinary women memorialized in the Women in the West Center, in Laramie.[14]

The decision by Wyoming's territorial legislature to grant women equal political rights accelerated women's involvement in national and state government for fifty years after its passage. Eliza Stewart Boyd was a remarkable woman with independence, talent, and confidence who made a lasting impact on the equality state.

Quick Reference Guide

Confident

The belief in one's ability to succeed by stimulating action through hard work, success, and even failure

If you bring the Grace perspective:

- Remember that displaying confidence is actually more important than having competence.
- The way to build confidence is through action.
- To demonstrate confidence, establish a physical presence by portraying a confident body posture. Practice sitting back and taking up space in a chair. Sit in a prominent place in the room, and always at the table.
- Speak with assurance, not thinking about how the idea might be shot down, and don't hesitate to speak up, even if your idea isn't fully formed.
- Stop apologizing and worrying about being liked. If you feel your confidence is shaky, try not to worry at that moment about being overly collaborative, as it may work against having a confident presence.
- Stop focusing on only competencies and focus on representing a point of view. Speaking factually about abilities or accomplishments is not bragging.
- Turn off the critical and negative self-talk.
- Adopt a growth mind-set and a belief that all skills can be developed through hard work and commitment, and that wherever you are is a starting point. This is an empowering position that demands a call to action.

If you bring the Grit perspective:

- Remember that you might have a tendency to be overconfident and overestimate your actual abilities.
- Self-awareness can help you to accurately assess your own strengths and areas of development.
- Self-awareness also can help in situations where others may lack confidence. Can you help facilitate opportunities for those with a Grace perspective to contribute and gain confidence?
- Practice your listening skills.

CHAPTER 8

Powerful

A great disparity exists between what it means to have power and being powerful, particularly for women. I personally have had a love-hate relationship with power my entire life. It was a soul-searching process to find the right personal experiences to share about power for this chapter. Maybe this is partly because, despite having a lifetime of career and personal accomplishments, I would not describe myself as powerful. Yet, I absolutely believe being powerful is a vital leadership behavior. It's also a complicated behavior that is tied to many others outlined in this book. Unfortunately, like confidence, a large body of evidence indicates that women misunderstand all that power can afford them.

Women's Ambivalent Relationship with Power

Many women have an ambivalent relationship with power. After the many discussions I have had with individuals on this subject, I've come to the conclusion that women often share my love-hate relationship with power. In some situations in my career, I have been in a position of power but, for some reason, had a hard time harnessing it to accomplish results. Other times, I have fully embraced and enjoyed all the benefits that power afforded, resulting in both a personal and organizational benefit. Women have fought hard throughout history for the right to be empowered. Why then are we so ambivalent about possessing it?

When I stepped into the role of advertising manager at HP, I obtained power through holding that position of influence. Advertising budgets were larger than any other marketing function, and, as the custodian of a considerable budget, I suddenly had increased access and visibility that others were not afforded. I will fully admit that I immediately embraced the opportunity and relished it. I enjoyed building relationships with key executives and having access that my prior positions had not permitted. I also liked that advertising strategy drove the majority of the other marketing activities and that this provided me with a seat at the decision-making table for the overall business strategy—meaning I had influence beyond marketing.

However, in embracing that power so enthusiastically, I began to recognize having power had other consequences that were not so fortunate. I noticed that my relationships with some of my closest work friends (both men and women) were a little bruised. We were not as close as we were before I had first taken the role, and this caused me to pause and reflect on the situation.

I thought about my behaviors and realized that, in some ways, the advantages I had gained in assuming the position of power had most likely been negatively reflected in my own actions. I could see where my friends might view some behaviors as arrogant, even though that was not my intention. After some thought, I approached my friends and talked openly about what I perceived to be the problem, along with my feelings, intentions, and a commitment to change.

The conversation was well received, and the relationships were repaired over time. This experience stayed with me, and I have worked diligently to fully embrace the benefits of having power while maintaining humility. This requires work and self-awareness. The challenge of balancing relationships while assuming power may have some bearing on the ambivalence women feel toward power and the complexities involved in embracing all that it offers.

The Potential Influence of Power

Power is defined many ways. Some describe it simply as having the ability to influence others. However, the idea of influence is a broader concept. In their book, *Management of Organizational Behavior*, Paul Hersey, Kenneth Blanchard, and Dewey Johnson composed what I find to be the most relevant definition of power: power is influence potential—the resource that enables a leader to gain commitment from others.[1]

Of course, gaining commitment is also critical to getting things done. As a leader I have found that pointing people in the right direction is the easy part of leadership; getting them to go there is much more difficult.

Power is an essential leadership behavior because power and leadership are tightly woven. An individual may exert power without being a leader; however, an individual cannot be a leader without possessing power. Leaders must apply power to achieve individual, team, and organizational goals. Leaders must be able to influence their followers to achieve greater performance, their superiors and peers to make important decisions, and stakeholders to ensure the strength of the organization.

Grace's Relationship to Power

Research indicates that many women, including those in influential leadership positions, may not correctly understand the definition of power. Researchers Anne Perschel and Jane Perdue interviewed 235 women in senior positions and found few appeared to have a complete understanding of power. Many used descriptors such as "power is passive," or "power is bestowed upon you. It is external to you," and "power is all about a 'decide and announce' culture."[2]

Perschel and Perdue's research also indicated that women were more than willing to step up into a position of power, but found that doing so might affect their likability. This caused them to believe they could not simultaneously hold a position of power and be liked. Because of their strong relationship focus, being forced to choose between being liked or having power affected both their view of power and their desire to obtain a position of power.

Power is viewed as a critical leadership skill for driving organizational results and effective leadership, and obtaining it requires ambition. Power, by definition, is closely related to ambition, or having an earnest desire to reach an achievement. A 2015 study commissioned by Pew Research Center indicated that women were more likely than men to say that having ambition was an essential trait for a leader: 57 percent of women and 48 percent of men said this is absolutely an essential skill.[3] Power and ambition are also closely related to possessing a strong internal drive toward actions, and therefore being results oriented. And, as already established above, these are also thought to be critical characteristics for effective leaders.

Grit's Relationship with Power

Grit has a familiar relationship with power because status is something he is conscious of every moment, and this is reflected in his everyday actions and words. In organizations, formal authority is derived from the position someone holds. Grit assumes that *actual* authority must be negotiated in every interaction. He is sensitive to the power dynamics of all interactions and understands the subtle signals that occur in everyday interactions that negotiate hierarchy. These sensitivities involve speaking in a way that resists being put in a one-down position, or conceded advantage, demonstrating confidence in actions, making statements as opposed to asking questions. Deborah Tannen also has noted another power negotiating behavior common to men that she refers to as "ritual opposition."[4]

Ritual opposition is when men present their own ideas in the most certain and absolute form they can and wait to see if they are challenged. I learned this from my husband: I have found that sometimes he powerfully states "facts" that are not exactly proven. I have also learned to call his bluff—which, according to Tannen, is what the challenge is about. I now understand that my husband is actually asking me to poke holes and find the weaknesses in his statement as a way of testing his idea.

This power play works well if everyone understands that this is the objective. I have found that many women tend to give up on their ideas if they are challenged in the workplace, or mistake being challenged for a true argument between individuals. The bottom line is that individuals who are uncomfortable with verbal opposition run the risk of appearing insecure about their ideas. This also has an effect on who is recognized as powerful.

As Tannen notes, people in powerful positions are likely to reward styles similar to their own. If most of the positions of power are held by Grit-oriented leaders, then those with a more Grace-focused style have an obvious disadvantage. Grace simply may not recognize the subtle cues of power behaviors that happen every day in the workplace.

Confidence and Power

A study from the U.K.'s ILM (Institute of Leadership and Management) found that the career ambitions of women managers lagged behind those of men. In general, women tended to set their sights lower and were more likely to limit ambitions to more junior ranks of management.[5] Embracing power is also further compounded for women because of their struggle with confidence. Research indicates that the combination of lacking confidence and ambition results in a lack of personal power. Personal power drives professional power, which in turn drives change in organizational stereotypes that will ultimately change the gender ratio at the top of organizations.

I spent my entire career downplaying my own personal desire for power, regardless of the fact that I am very results driven as an individual, because I thought it said something undesirable about my personal character. I shunned what I saw as a negative statement about me that having power conveyed. I focused purely on the negative association of ambition related to wielding power over others, and thinking that possessing power meant I also possessed a large ego. I did not understand that having power and ambition could be a positive source of power for others and that I could empower followers and peers by using my own personal power.

A lack of confidence early in my career likely prevented me from pursuing a position of power, and I am not alone. A study by Perschel and Perdue found confidence to be a key barrier to power with self-confidence mentioned repeatedly as an internal limiting factor.[6]

Fulfillment and Power

Women lacking power don't believe it can fulfill their wants. To help women reshape their misinterpretations of what it means to be powerful requires those currently in positions of power to communicate its value to women who lack it. A 2014 report released by the Center for Talent Innovation (CTI), *Women Want Five Things*, found that the majority of women (60 percent of women in the U.S., 65 percent in the U.K., and 49 percent in Germany) between the ages of thirty-five and fifty perceive that the burdens of having a powerful position outweigh the benefits.[7]

Yet findings from the same study also show that women who possess power in their current roles are more likely than women without it to get what they want from their careers. The study explored what appears to be a significant disconnect between women's expectations of having a powerful job and the realities and opportunities that having such a position affords.

Not believing or understanding the benefits of power has an effect on the women who aspire to obtain leadership roles. The study revealed that, despite being highly ambitious, less than one-fifth (17 percent) of these professional women ages thirty-five to fifty in the U.S. aspire to achieve a position of power.[8]

Instead, women view an executive role—a position that affords power—as delivering a hefty salary but little else of what they want in their careers. The study concluded that what drives women and what inspires them to remain fully engaged and on track for leadership roles is a five-point value proposition: women want to flourish, excel, reach for meaning and purpose, be empowered and empower others, and earn well.

A closer look at the individual components of this value proposition exposes how women misunderstand power in the context of their desires. Women who possess power have distinctly different perceptions of its merits compared with women who do not.

Flourishing

The CTI study found that women tend to flourish when they feel they have support, impact, and the ability to self-actualize. Flourishing is grounded in physical and emotional health and in having freedom and autonomy. When women have a real measure of control, they can manage competing demands in ways that sustain their physical and spiritual well-being, replenish their energy, and fulfill their wishes.

Fifty-eight percent of women who have power (defined as influence validated by title or status) in the U.S. and 36 percent of women with power in the U.K. reported having the ability to flourish as defined above. Only 18 percent of women without power in the U.S. and 22 percent of women without power in the U.K., however, expected that an executive position would allow them to flourish.

Excelling

The study defined "excel" as meeting an intellectual challenge that fosters continued growth toward personal mastery in a domain of knowledge or area of expertise. To maintain their drive for excellence women need an approving audience. This reveals the importance of recognition by peers or supervisors as a motivator for ambitious women.[9]

Eighty-seven percent of women surveyed in the U.S. who possess power reported being able to excel in their roles, an expectation held by 70 percent of women without power—illustrating that women generally underestimate how power will benefit them.[10]

Reaching for Meaning and Purpose

The study found that women find work meaningful when it enables them to model success for others and exceed expectations—their own, and those of their family or community. It was important for women to achieve stretch goals set before them or their team and to have a lasting impact in their profession, field, or community. Women find work particularly meaningful when it helps to advance causes important to them such as improving lives through health and education, advancing social justice, and healing the planet.[11]

More than a third of women with power (63 percent in the U.S., 40 percent in the U.K., and 35 percent in Germany) said they have the opportunity to reach for meaning and purpose through their careers. The majority of women without power (74 percent in the U.S., 72 percent in the U.K., and 78 percent in Germany) expected, however, that an executive position would not provide them with meaning and purpose.[12]

Empowerment

Empowerment was also important to women in the CTI study, and my own research validates this finding. Women who ultimately land senior positions seek out sponsors, such as senior colleagues, who are willing to support them and advocate for their next big opportunity. They also seek out protégés or high-achieving junior colleagues who might deepen their capabilities, extend their reach, and burnish their own brand under the respondents' guidance and support.[13]

Sixty-one percent of women holding power positions in the U.S. and 35 percent in the U.K. said they enjoyed the ability to empower others and be empowered themselves, while the majority of women without power (86 percent in the U.S. and U.K.) believed that holding an executive position would not afford them the ability to empower others and be empowered.

Earning Well

The fifth point of the five-point value proposition was to earn well. In the study, women said it was important to them to attain financial security as well as financial independence, but also to sustain a comfortable lifestyle for themselves, their offspring, and their parents. Women without power were inclined to believe that, with an executive position, they would earn well; sadly, the majority of women in positions of power reported that they do not earn well.[14] Of course, genderwage gap statistics support the truth behind this perception.

According to the Institute for Women's Policy Research, women represent half the workforce and share in the family contribution as an equal or main breadwinner in four out of ten families, yet still on average earn considerably less than men. The gender wage gap in the United States has not seen significant improvements in recent years. In 2014, women who were full-time workers made only 71 cents for every dollar earned by men, a gender wage gap of 29 percent. Women, on average, earn less than men in virtually every occupation for which there is sufficient earnings data to calculate an earnings ratio.[15] Obviously there is still much work to be done in the area of pay equity for women, even for women in powerful positions.

Embracing Power as a Grace-Focused Leader

I can say from first-hand experience as the top executive of a global company, having power enabled me to accomplish the value-proposition points in CTI's study: flourishing, finding meaning and purpose, excelling in my own personal growth and overall career growth, and being empowered and empowering others.

When I first took the role at Performics, I was concerned, because I did not have prior experience running a company. Combined with my personal feelings of ambiguity toward power, ego, status, and ambition, I had to work constantly to subdue the warning voices in my head. I honestly did not expect to enjoy the role as much as I did. I can remember initially having self-deprecating conversations with others about assuming the role. Instead of being proud of my new role, I found myself apologizing for it, or providing others with a detailed disclaimer about why I took it.

As I settled into the position, I more than enjoyed it—I *loved* it. I stopped apologizing. Similar to how women in CTI study described their satisfaction around the five-point value proposition, I flourished in the role of CEO because when I saw an opportunity (good or bad), I had the positional power to do something about it. It was incredibly gratifying to turn the company around and ignite the spirit of my employees in the process. This was how I learned to own personal power.

Perhaps my negative view of power originated from personal experiences in which I saw individuals with power misuse it. As head of the company, I reminded myself that this was not how I would choose to lead. I had the ultimate authority to build meaning and purpose into every action that I took, every single day.

This was not about having power *over* others, but working *with* them in the pursuit of something great. It was about working hard to monitor, maintain, and preserve relationships to further organizational goals. Empowering others was a vital component of my personal approach to Grace-focused leadership. I strove to be someone who inspired people to want to be better, provided them with something greater to believe in, and empowered them to grow as individuals. I discovered that I could accomplish all of this while being the down-to-earth, humble, open, and approachable person I have always been.

Embracing power didn't mean changing my values or my personality. I was able to create my own power by leveraging the strengths associated with Grace. Having power enabled me to take action, exude confidence, and be decisive and inspiring. This applied not just at work but throughout my whole life, with my family and in my community. I want everyone to understand the importance of embracing power, and to recognize that they can establish power on their own terms without sacrificing effectiveness or abandoning a Grace style of leadership.

Choosing to Have Personal Power

The first step toward becoming a leader is choosing to have power. This insight around the importance of embracing my own brand of personal power was further reinforced when I made the decision to leave my role at Performics and move to Twitter, where I assumed a position that had less power and authority. The Twitter position was still an important leadership role within the organization, but marketing was distributed throughout the organization and lacked overall leadership. I told myself going in (and this was affirmed by others) that I could still have influence and make a difference, and that having overall power and authority wasn't important.

Looking back, it was clear that I had already forgotten about the downside of not having power and authority. In my new role, I found myself in the frustrating position of seeing clearly what needed to change, presumably with the credentials to make it so, but lacking the positional authority to make it happen. I discovered that I needed to embrace my own personal power, which included recognizing the superpower women have through our relationship acumen and transformational leadership style.

Women's Superpower: Relationship Acumen

Women innately possess the ability to drive power through relationships. This is a critical leadership skill that all leaders, not just women, will be required to possess to achieve success in the future.[16] Women should leverage this advantage toward securing a leadership position. Studies show that women are rated higher on factors such as collaboration, teamwork, and relationship building—which are all valuable skills when applying power through relationships. Women have an opportunity to create an evolved definition of power, a more "transformational" style of power, a more collaborative, engaging, and inspirational way to lead—the power of Grace.

Transformational leaders exercise power differently than transactional leaders. Transactional leaders tend to use positional power, rewarding and punishing others on the basis of their position, and exercising hierarchical power. The entire premise of transactional leadership is about holding power over others. Transformational leaders, in contrast, use relationship power to inspire and motivate others. The goal of transformational leadership is to enrich and empower others and to use that energy to propel the organization forward.[17]

In general, women feel more comfortable using relationship power than positional power. According to research by Alice Eagly, quoted in "The Leadership Styles of Women and Men" in the *Journal of Social Issues*, female managers, more than male managers, manifest the following leadership attributes related to relationships: motivating their followers to feel respect and pride because of their association with them, showing optimism and excitement about future goals, and attempting to develop and mentor followers and attend to their individual needs.[18]

In the future, transformational power will become the preferred style for organizations. Markets are now global, with competitors entering markets from unlikely places. And leaders at the top of hierarchies have less information to make timely decisions than people who are closest to customers and influencers. This calls for organizations that have a broader distribution of power.

Transformational Power

According to an article in *Harvard Business Review*, organizations that allow employees to voice their concerns freely have increased retention and stronger overall performance. However, despite efforts focused on improving communications up and down the organizational hierarchy, often a fear of consequences still exists for speaking up where there is a more transactional approach to leadership, including embarrassment and lost promotions, and a perceived sense of futility or the belief that speaking up won't make a difference. The authors of the article recommend softening the power cues in order to obtain honest, open communications from employees.[19] This is where Grace has a clear advantage over Grit. Employees feel safe sharing their insights and communicating openly when they see leaders advocating for them and truly caring about them as individuals.

Transformational power is about sharing information in an open and transparent way, throughout the entire organization. Our world is changing rapidly. There is an opportunity to redefine the meaning of power in order to better reflect the inclusive thinking required in today's complex, fast-paced global environment. Those who lead with Grace can be instrumental in driving this change. If we are to move forward as a society, we need to make it acceptable for people of any gender to exercise this type of leadership power. We need to make it okay for men and women to put down the burden of traditional command and control leadership that is about having power over others.

Power Personified: Cindy Gallop

There are women who possess ambition and power and use it to help propel other women forward, despite the odds. Cindy Gallop is someone I would describe as powerful with a capitol *P*. Cindy graduated from Somerville College in Oxford, England, and began her career in marketing and advertising, heading up the U.S. office of ad agency Bartle Bogle Hegarty, in New York, in 1998. She was named Advertising Woman of the Year in 2003 and is the founder and CEO of IfWeRanTheWorld.com, a website that promotes taking doable micro-actions to effect the change you want to see in the world. The website was launched at TED2010.

Cindy uses her power to influence in each and every communication—in person, through social media, etc. She is a frequent speaker and began to inspire larger audiences by sharing her passions at key events. At TED2009, where she was just an audience member, Cindy gave a short presentation that became one of the event's most talked-about moments, even years later. Speaking from her own experience, she argued that hardcore pornography had distorted the way a generation of young men thinks about sex, and talked about how she was fighting back with the launch of a website to correct the myths being propagated.

While her talk's graphic content may not have been suitable for every listener, she passionately raised important issues that have become her purpose. Cindy's desire to drive healthy attitudes and behaviors around sex led to her launching Make Love Not Porn, an online membership community that shares real-world sex videos and open, healthy conversations around sex. Both projects are representative of Cindy's core beliefs that the best and most profitable businesses focus on doing good in the world, and that real change occurs from the bottom up, not the top down. She firmly believes that everyone is empowered to make a difference, and should embrace their personal power to do so.

Cindy's projects are bold and controversial, and, although she is a staunch advocate for women, she is fearless in encouraging conversations about the importance of having both genders represented. Her experience in advertising heightened her awareness of the issues facing women in companies where a male leadership style is the standard, as she explained in an interview with *Marketing* magazine: "We live in a world where the default setting is always male."

In response to being asked whether men get this, Gallop noted the gap between social and corporate change when it comes to gender: "The entire corporate structure was designed and built up at a time when it was believed that only men would ever go to work and there would always be a woman at home taking care of everything else. Everything's changed. Corporate systems and structures haven't."

Cindy embraces the notion that men find working with women awkward because women have different mind-sets, perspectives. and even, in many cases, a different overall approach to solving business problems. "Women challenge the status quo because we are never it," Cindy said in the interview.

Cindy's power platform is much broader than just gender. She believes that the benefit of having diversity in business applies equally to race, ethnicity, sexuality, and other social factors and that unique ideas arise from completely different backgrounds.[20]

Cindy inspires us all to remember that power comes from within, conviction comes from power and truth, and that these build confidence that makes it easy to stand fearlessly and assume a position of power for what you believe in.

As Cindy's story illustrates, women who want to change the power game for themselves and for others must find a way through and around the internal and external obstacles in their way. They must also support one another in reshaping a world where having power over others is no longer the default approach to powerful leadership. Embracing the transformational style of leadership can be a big first step in this direction.

Power is a complex and sometimes painful leadership behavior, but critical to leadership success. Women have a unique opportunity to change the meaning of power in the workplace by embracing Grace and demonstrating that the Grit approach to power is not enough.

For women seeking to embrace power, discovering their authentic selves and leveraging relationship power are important stepping-stones. Similar to confidence, embracing power might seem at odds with a relationship-focused communications style, but, to be successful in business, women must not be afraid or hesitant. Instead, it's critical for women to leverage all of the leadership behaviors outlined in this book in order to become remarkable, courageous leaders who are inspiring, driven, decisive, confident, resilient, and powerful. Being decisive, driven, and confident are especially critical leadership behaviors to owning personal power. Women shouldn't be afraid to speak up, stand up, and not wait to be handed the opportunity, but rather just to take it.

Developing Power Through Networking

I've mentioned the importance of establishing and maintaining a strong network several times throughout *Grace Meets Grit*, but this is particularly relevant to developing personal power. I have found it critical to my own career success. Having a group of supporters who can be independent sounding boards has been invaluable many times, and I force myself to carve out time for this activity.

I also believe it's critical to support other women. This means demonstrating support for those on all sides: below, beside, and above. If we don't support each other, how can we ask others to support us?

Having power is truly where Grace meets Grit. It's not about having one or the other leadership styles but about having both. Now is the time for women to embrace power and facilitate changes that will transform their leadership.

Historical Inspiration: The Women of Wyoming

The first to gain the power of voting in the United States

If power has the potential to influence, then the first step to women's having broad influence was through the right to vote. As mentioned in previous chapters, Wyoming was the first place in the United States to grant women voting privileges, in 1869. Women in Wyoming achieved this power long before other states and even many civilized countries. According to papers at the Jackson Hole Historical Society, Wyoming was not yet a state and still largely unpopulated when its territorial representatives voted for the measure that declared "every woman of the age of 21 years, residing in this Territory, may at every election to be holden under the law thereof, cast her vote."[21]

Unlike in other states and countries, there were no organized suffrage demonstrations or public displays advocating for this change. Women just kept a vigil outside Governor John A. Campbell's office until he signed the bill into law.

There is even speculation that the Wyoming lawmakers didn't truly have women's rights in mind when they first proposed the bill. Although no record was kept of what they did discuss as they were debating the bill, some facts can be gleaned from newspaper articles and from people's memories reported years later. These indicated that some people at the time wondered if the bill was a political maneuver designed to advance partisan causes—a publicity stunt to get more people to settle in the remote territory, including women. At the time, there were six adult men in the territory for every adult woman, and few children.

In 1890, the right of women to vote in Wyoming was in jeopardy when the U.S. Congress strongly opposed women's suffrage and threatened to withhold statehood for the territory unless it repealed the law. Women lobbied vigorously against the threat, causing officials to send back an unwaveringly worded telegram stating that Wyoming would remain out of the Union for one hundred years rather than join without women's suffrage.

On July 10, 1890, President Benjamin Harrison signed the bill ushering in Wyoming as the nation's "Equality State." Eliza A. "Grandma" Swain of Laramie claimed the honor of being the first women to cast a ballot in 1870. Although Susan B. Anthony's call for Eastern women to migrate to Wyoming went largely ignored, national suffragette champions Anthony and Elizabeth Cady Stanton traveled to the Equality State on the newly completed Transcontinental Railroad in 1871.

Other Western states followed Wyoming's lead, and subsequently the West became the first region where women had the power to lead and influence through their vote. Eastern states, including New York, did not achieve that until 1917.

For most women, the right to participate fully in their community's politics became a fact of life as necessary as working, eating, or breathing. Granting women voting power early on likely catapulted the other extraordinary number of Wyoming firsts for women, including, as already mentioned, the appointment of Ester Hobart Morris as first justice of the peace in 1870; Jackson Hole's becoming the first town in the U.S. to be entirely governed by women, in 1920; and Nellie Tayloe Ross's being elected the nation's first woman governor in 1924.

Along with those firsts are the first all-woman jury and the first woman bailiff in the U.S., Mary Atkinson, in 1870, Pauline Bayer, and so many others whose stories have not been publicized. It is unfortunate, that despite the "Equality State's" progressive approach to women in leadership in its early days, Wyoming has sadly lost its edge in advocating for women in power. In 2016 it ranked forty-sixth out of fifty in the percentage of women in state legislatures.

Quick Reference Guide

Powerful

The ability to flourish, excel, reach for meaning and purpose, be empowered and empower others, and earn well

If you bring the Grace perspective:

- Step up to power confidently. Leaders need power to achieve individual, team, and organizational goals, so embracing power is vital for leadership success.
- Be authentic. Define power by your standards. That sometimes means fighting the traditional Grit approach.
- Leverage your advantage in relationship power to influence others, creating positive organizational and business value.
- Choose power. You don't have to choose between power and being liked—you can have both.
- Remember that others with a Grace perspective may be sensitive to the traditional hierarchy aligned to power of position, which can sometimes make chain-of-command situations uncomfortable.
- Network. Surround yourself with support and support others, especially the women beside, above, and below you.

If you bring the Grit perspective:

- Remember that power is about influence potential, which means relationships are just as important as status.
- Challenge the traditional definitions of power and leadership and help raise awareness about the benefits of collaboration, emotional intelligence, relationship building, and intuitive thinking.

- Champion open, honest conversations about the differences between Grace and Grit power and how they can be leveraged for the benefit of the entire organization.
- Maintain an empathetic and relationship-focused team approach.
- Remember that, although Grace's power may look different than Grit's, the power of relationships may even be more effective.

CHAPTER 9

Resilient

Like so many other people today, my home life is just as important as my work life. My husband and I have a blended family of three wonderful children who I'm proud to say have grown into remarkable human beings. They are all very different in their individual ways. The younger two, a daughter and a son, are from my first marriage, and the oldest son is from my husband's first marriage. Rob and I have been married now for nearly twenty years, so remembering that there was a time before our relationship, and before our blended family, sometimes feels surreal.

I am thankful Rob and I are together today. We have an amazing partnership. He is my best friend and the love of my life. He has been the only father my children know, and he is my biggest fan. As I mentioned in chapter 7, it was with his support and encouragement that I threw my hat in the ring for the CEO role at Performics. He had more confidence in my abilities than I did at the time, and he believed in me enough to sacrifice his own career to be at home for the kids, knowing that my taking the CEO role meant I could not be there. At that time, the kids weren't young, but even in high school—or maybe, *especially* in high school—kids require someone to be at home, and he provided it when I was on the road.

My time with Rob has built my confidence. The earlier life I shared with my first husband was a test of my resilience. It's a time I don't often talk about, with a relationship that ended in divorce, but not as a result of circumstances that normally precipitate the end of a marriage.

My first husband, Dwayne, was older than me. Today, I am nearly the age he was when, together, we decided that divorce was the most financially prudent path.

Up until the time my daughter was six and my son was two, we had a very normal married life. Sometime around my son's second birthday Dwayne began acting strangely. I missed it at first—everyone missed the little signs in the beginning. Dwayne was born with an ambitious work ethic. It was not unusual for him to work full days on Saturdays. He didn't do it to brag about the hours, but because he took great pride in his work as the owner of his own automotive repair business. His business was only a few years old and grew organically by word of mouth from every satisfied customer. Working on Saturdays was about pleasing a customer and getting their car back to them earlier than promised.

Subtle behavior changes are sometimes difficult to notice at first. Over several months, I discovered that, while he appeared to be going to work, Dwayne wasn't really completing tasks. Because he was self-employed and only he really knew what was going on from day-to-day, it took a long time for me to figure this out. I had noticed that several customers returned perplexed that the repairs he claimed to have completed on their cars hadn't been done, even though Dwayne had documented them and returned the car. Many customers were friends and long-time acquaintances, and were forgiving... at first.

There were other signs of something wrong, including Dwayne's starting to pace around the house. This, too, was gradual at first until it became nearly constant striding, like a caged cat, often accompanied by strange muttering under his breath. Over time he also seemed to fade in and out of being present, unable to concentrate or focus. After several months spent visiting numerous specialists and undergoing copious tests, we finally had an unexpected and devastating diagnosis. I will never forget sitting in the neurologist's office the day we learned what was happening in Dwayne's brain. The neurologist showed us the MRI results, explaining the image illuminated "brain shrinkage," and he spoke of the "frontal lobe implications" multiple times.

This was completely unfamiliar to me and I sat stunned, trying to comprehend what it meant for Dwayne, who sat silently. The neurologist ushered us out of his office, quickly explaining he was due at his next appointment, even though I didn't really understand what he was telling me at the time. He must have read the confusion on my face because he stuffed a number of brochures about Alzheimer's disease into my hands as I walked out the door. I sat in the car and looked at the printed handouts in confusion because not one physician had ever mentioned Alzheimer's to me, ever. This was before the Internet, so the brochures were our only access to information.

I drove Dwayne home and returned to work, where I placed a call to our family doctor, who had helped us start the quest for a diagnosis. I requested that he consult with all of the specialists we had visited and translate the verdict in a way we could understand. Through his help, we came to understand the significance and implications of the test results. Dwayne had an early form of frontotemporal dementia, better known then as Pick's disease. Pick's is named after Arnold Pick, a professor of psychiatry from the University of Prague who first discovered and described the disease in 1892.[1] Because the disease is concentrated in the frontal lobes of the brain, where all critical thinking occurs, our doctor informed us that incapacitation would occur quickly, and he advised us to prepare soon—whatever that meant.

I remember thinking to myself, "Prepare? How? What for?" And, of course, I asked why: "Why my husband? Why us? Why now?" Why would this happen when he had so much to look forward to? Dwayne would not get to see our two young children grow up.

Denial didn't last long. Knowing the diagnosis brought into focus the rapid cognitive degeneration progressing daily. There were moments when he seemed to be the normal Dwayne, and progressively more moments when the person I knew was gone. We took advantage of the good moments and talked about everything: his hopes, his wishes, how to prepare. Most worrying to both of us was the financial burden of caring for two young children, given the expected costs of his treatment.

We both understood that, while the disease would likely progress quickly, the experts could not tell us how long Dwayne would live. They did tell us that Pick's disease would not be the ultimate cause of death.

Rather, we were to expect progressive deterioration of the mind that would ultimately implicate the body. But no one knew how long this would take. Dwayne was young and so it was a reasonable speculation that he would spend years in an institution requiring expensive care.

Together we decided a divorce was the best course of action to protect the financial resources for the family. He wanted us to move on, and we knew we needed to act quickly, while he was deemed competent to make the decision. If we chose to wait until he was not mentally competent, then state law dictated that he would need to be institutionalized for a minimum of six years before divorce papers could be filed. At that time, an attorney would be appointed to represent him to argue against me for resources.

Dwayne wanted to act while he had control of his decisions. The thought of someone he didn't know speculating his wishes was particularly disturbing to him, and seemed a worse course than divorce, which would provide legal separation of assets and ensure that I would have sufficient resources to support our children. It was the most financially responsible choice.

However logical, this did not make the decision any easier. I cannot, even today, imagine how difficult even discussing it must have been for him. He did not share this with me at the time, but it must have been terrifying.

I cared for Dwayne in our home as long as I could. Debilitation progressed quickly. Only a few months following the diagnosis, I became worried about leaving him home alone during the day when I went to work.

I was working full time at HP, providing care for my children and for Dwayne, and was determined to navigate the unexpected circumstances as they emerged. Thankfully, my coworkers at HP were the closest thing I had to family nearby, and they were wonderful. Volunteers took turns dropping off dinner at our home five days a week. A trusted work friend, along with Dwayne's brother, guided me through the rough time when he finally had to be institutionalized.

Twenty years later, as I look back on this time of my life, I'm not sure how I managed through it all. Somehow I just kept moving forward; no matter what obstacle presented itself, I kept on keeping on. I'm sure the fact that I had two young children to support sustained me more than any other factor.

This experience taught me that I have resilience—even during times when I feel vulnerable, tired, disenchanted, afraid, or uncertain, I know I possess the purest form of resilience: true grit. If I had to choose a single leadership quality that has contributed most to my career accomplishments and success in life overall, resilience would be the one.

Traits of Resilient Leaders

Companies, businesses, teams, and individuals all fail at some point. Leaders can choose to allow fear of failure to paralyze them, which ultimately may stagnate growth. There are leaders who have an uncanny ability to overcome challenges—and even learn from the tough times by adapting and leading their organizations forward.

Bouncing Forward

Resilience is a critical leadership behavior that is vital, not only in tragic life situations but also in the workplace. Often described as a personal quality that predisposes individuals to bounce back in the face of challenges or loss, resilient leaders do more than bounce back—they bounce forward. With speed and elegance, resilient leaders take action in response to new and ever-changing realities, even as they maintain the essential operations of the organizations they lead.[2]

Not only do resilient leaders quickly get their mojo back, but, because they understand that the status quo is unsustainable, they also use the challenges they face to move the organization forward in unique and innovative ways. Living in an urgent workplace situation for a few weeks or even few months is one thing, but what about facing a challenging business situation, such as financial shortcomings or failure for six months, a year, or even longer?

When I first took the leadership reins at Performics, the company had been in a new business drought for well over a year. Almost always invited to participate in big pitches, Performics could get a seat at the table but could not seem to win. In the agency business, there is no prize for second place.

A focus on driving new business requires a huge investment in time and energy from a large group of individuals across multiple departments.

It takes focus and heart and, after numerous losses, maintaining those becomes more and more difficult. To make matters worse, at Performics, existing clients were leaving as well. This was having a very negative effect on company morale. The solution involved healing some of the emotional baggage between departments, while simultaneously revising the pitch approach, process, and value proposition of the company. It was my job to navigate Performics through this challenge. This is what resilience as a leadership characteristic is all about.

Being Positive and Focused Yet Flexible

To thrive through the disruptive, fast-paced changes occurring in today's workplace environments, transformative leaders need to be positive, focused, and yet flexible. In times of stress, having a strong sense of self-esteem, being empathetic, and managing the give and take of interpersonal interactions are all crucially important for transformative leaders, especially while their company is recovering from disruptions. As the company leader, I had to be the rock that backed up the losing team, while fixing those things that prevented us from taking home the win.

It's a fine balance, and careful consideration was required to manage all of the factors influencing the business challenges while shoring up the fragile morale. Resilience often means putting your own emotions aside while staying in tune with the emotions of those you lead and having genuine empathy for followers. Developing the skill to manage emotions gives resilient leaders the ability to recover quickly and tap into strength, even when stretched beyond their normal limits. This is where Grace can tap into her emotional IQ as a resilient leader.

Transformative Leaders Can Sense Organizational Resilience

Transformative leaders are honest and transparent. Less effective leaders are so risk averse that they often put on blinders to avoid seeing the truth in precarious situations. Still others are so pessimistic about any turn of fortune that they ignore opportunities for growth. But a leader who has the relationship focus to stay attuned to what is happening throughout the organization recognizes both opportunities and harbingers of disaster. Such a leader monitors signals of flagging resilience in her organization and reignites the spirit of those at all levels of the organization.

According to Steven Snyder, the author of *Leadership and the Art of Struggle*, "resilience is an exceptionally difficult leadership skill, requiring individuals to embrace the courage required to confront painful realities, the faith that there will be a solution when one isn't immediately evident, and the tenacity to carry on despite a nagging gut feeling that the situation is hopeless."[3]

Rosabeth Moss Kanter, Harvard Business School professor and director of the Harvard Advanced Leadership Initiative, claims no one is completely immune to avoiding challenging situations, so having the ability to tap into resilience is a definite plus. The real skill, according to Kanter, is the ability to recover from mistakes and bounce back. Having flexibility alone is not enough. Endurance is critical for individuals to learn from their mistakes and adapt.

The Four Values Resilient Leaders Foster

Kanter defines leaders who possess resilience skills as having four foundational cornerstones: confidence, accountability (taking responsibility and showing remorse), collaboration (supporting others in reaching a common goal), and initiative (being driven and focusing on positive steps and improvements). These four factors underpin the resilience of individuals, teams, and organizations that keep moving forward in the face of challenge. They also should sound familiar, as we have already covered confidence and initiative (drive) in previous chapters in this book.

For Laura Kofoid, the owner and cofounder of Laudi Vidni, the custom handbag company referenced in chapter 5, resilience was instrumental in getting her business off the ground as well as her bouncing forward despite personal and family health setbacks along the way. Laura's dream was to build a company that would enable women to design a handbag from the ground up, first choosing its shape, then leather colors and textures, and finally gold or silver hardware. She believes a handbag is personally tied to a woman's identity. A customizable handbag empowers women to create a part of their brand that everyone can see. In fact, individuality is even reflected in the company name: Laudi Vidni is "individual" spelled backwards.

However, designing handbags from scratch, one at a time, defies the traditional manufacturing process. Before Laura and her partner could even pursue funding to get their concept off the ground, she needed to find a factory that would build handbags one at a time. She told me she visited forty different factories and each time was told firmly "no." But this did not deter her; she was confident that her product idea was sound, and she was endlessly persistent in the pursuit of bringing it to life. She used the information she gathered during each unsuccessful visit to be more prepared for the next meeting. Her persistence paid off: at the fortieth factory visit, she got a "yes."

Personal and Professional Benefits of Resilience

I asked Laura Kofoid how she maintains her resilience in the face of what she's gone through.

"I had to look up the definition of resilient because while I intuitively feel resilient," she responded, "I wasn't really sure exactly what it meant. The definition includes flexible, durable, hardwearing, strong, sturdy, tough, quick to recover, irrepressible…and buoyant. I am all of that."

Laura agreed that resilience has had everything to do with the success of Laudi Vidni, though she admitted she might not be the poster child start-up CEO:

> I joke with people that my book title will be "I Am Not Mark Zuckerberg." Laudi Vidni did not emerge in my consciousness. It was not a runaway success. I am not in my twenties. I am not rich beyond my wildest dreams.
>
> When we were initially looking for factories to make bags for our then-new concept, I was turned down by a countless number of factories, each one explaining to me why custom handbags could never happen. One factory owner went so far as to tell me, "over my dead body, will you ever find anyone to make you one purse at a time."

But now we've sold more than five thousand bags and have two factories making bags one at a time—and a third pitching to make bags one at a time.

The rocky start Laura faced in finding a factory willing to make one bag at a time and securing investors who would fund the project turned out to be just the beginning of the bumps Laura would experience launching her young business. As she explains:

Laudi Vidni and I have endured too many disappointments and hardships to mention: A theft of all our bags the Monday before Thanksgiving—check. A potential investor who cut the deal after the term sheet expired and consequently saddled us with $60,000 in legal fees—check. A product that didn't meet expectations—check. A very expensive website that didn't work—check, check...check.

So, we kept our nose to the grindstone and fixed our problems one by one. And now, today, finally I feel as though we've created something of value—flexible, hardwearing, sturdy, irrepressible.

But business is not the only place where Laura has endured many ups and downs. When I asked about surmounting her personal challenges, Laura became introspective, explaining that becoming resilient was never an achievement she actively sought:

I really, really wish I didn't have to be resilient. As a young girl dreaming of my life, I did not think, "Wow, I hope I'm resilient." Rather I dreamed of being glamorous, joyful, funny. But my life has forced resilience on me.

My husband is a two-time brain-tumor survivor. That seems like enough cancer for one family, right? Apparently, not for the universe, because, in 2013, I was diagnosed with two types of cancer—both treatable, neither as grave as brain cancer...but cancer nonetheless. And I speak from experience when I say that cancer sucks.

She paused to reflect, then summed up where these trials had taken her:

That cancer double-whammy sent me into a tailspin because it just wasn't fair. I spent about a year grieving for the unfairness of it all. And then that was that. Today I live in gratitude for all I have and in denial of the uncertainty of life. Quick (sort of) to recover, irrepressible, buoyant.

Self-Prioritizing to Become Resilient

Laura is quick to point out how important it is to prioritize self as a key component of maintaining resilience:

I have always had a clear priority for family time, sleep, and exercise. I have a wonderful husband, twenty-seven years of marriage, and two kids who are now thirteen and eighteen, and I have a physical need to spend time with them . . . not *all* my time with them, but time. I pretty much need seven to nine hours of sleep at night.

And I exercise—yoga, strength training, walking, tennis—most every day. I have done all of these things for most of my life. And yet, in spite of this, I was very stressed about my business and that affected all aspects of my life. Is it the "reason" I got cancer? I don't know. But I have made even more of an effort, since cancer, to live well . . . to read, to listen to classical music or jazz, to laugh with friends, to drink more wine.

In the end there's no question that being resilient has been essential to Laura's success in business, in her marriage, and in her life. Resilience is integral to who she is as a person, a woman, and a leader:

I tell my kids, "Success isn't what life gives you. Success is what you do with what life gives you." No one gets through life (professional or personal) without a major hurdle or twelve. In that way, resilience or determination or perseverance, is critical to success.

However, I also think success lies in knowing when to quit. Sticking with something just because it's all you know how to do or it's how it has always been done, isn't a recipe for success. Yet it's often hard to tell if the path you're taking is resilience or pig-headedness—willful determination or stupidity?

I have asked myself this question often in the experience of building my business. I think many smart people would have called it quits by now and they wouldn't be wrong. But my gut has told me to keep going so I do.

The Natural Resilience of Women

My own story and Laura Kofoid's are testaments to the resilience that women can possess when faced with daunting challenges. Resilience is a superpower that comes from within, and it seems women have an advantage in possessing resilience from the moment they take their first breath. For years, doctors have marveled over the fact that girls born prematurely have better odds of thriving than boys.

In fact, a 2006 study published in the journal *Pediatrics* found that black baby girls born weighing 2.2 pounds or less are more than twice as likely to survive as white baby boys born at the same weight. Analyzing data from more than five thousand premature births, the researchers pinpointed a link between gender and race and the survival rates of babies born at extremely low weights.[4]

The same study validated prior research that indicated baby girls of both races had the strongest advantage when born weighing less than 1,000 grams, about two pounds. In fact, girls had nearly twice the odds of surviving as baby boys did.

Other research indicates that the quality of resilience in young girls appears to continue through their teenage years or early twenties. Academics at Leeds Metropolitan University tested around 1,500 students at the start of their first year of college to see if levels of psychological resilience or "the capacity of individuals to adapt to new challenges" affected academic performance. Those who were judged as "resilient," after undergoing a four-stage analysis called the Connor Davison

Resilience Scale (CD-RISC), were more likely to do well in their first year studies.[5]

The Leeds Metropolitan University research indicated that this trend was much more pronounced for female students than for male ones. This study also indicated that women are more resilient under stress. The capacity of female students to perform effectively despite the negative effects of stress may be attributed to the female preference to cope by adopting relation-based responses. Women were more likely to leverage their innate Grace qualities and would reach out to others to ask for help and seek support when stressed. While females tended also to display anxiety, they valued social connections where they would talk about their feelings and share sadness—all characteristics of relational resilience, according to the researchers.

In contrast, male students displayed a reluctance to seek help, collaboration, or support, especially during times of stress. Researchers speculated that these behaviors could represent the male tendency to cope by attributing failure externally to preserve an image of self-reliance and invulnerability. Ironically, avoiding appearing vulnerable actually made these young men more vulnerable. While this study was limited to students, it is supporting evidence of how, once again, innate gender communication styles affect leadership behaviors.

I have seen a similar situation play out in the workplace. I have noticed on multiple occasions that Grit leaders prefer to work independently and are reluctant to ask for support or help, particularly in stressful situations. Of the four cornerstones of resilience—confidence, accountability, collaboration, and initiative—Grit-focused leaders often overlook or avoid one, collaboration, in their desire to appear confident. This behavior supports Grit's relentless desire to maintain status but can cause a number of unintended detrimental consequences.

While the more stoic, independent Grit approach is often the expected leadership style, it's important to remember that collaboration is key to building and maintaining organizational resilience. Leveraging the relationship-focused power of Grace at stressful times can benefit individual leaders and the entire organization.

The Resilience of Women Under Stress

As a leader, the true test of resilience comes during high stress days, weeks, and even months. Women tend to react to stress differently than men. When under stress, women do not lose their desire to connect with others. Studies indicate that, during stressful situations, women have greater emotional intelligence than men. A recent study found that stressed men become more self-centered and less able to distinguish their own emotions and intentions from those of other people.

For women, the exact opposite is true. This study, conducted by researchers at the Social Cognitive Neuroscience Unit of the University of Vienna, along with the University of Freiburg, was surprised by this outcome. The initial hypothesis was that stress would cause all individuals to become more egocentric, because taking a self-centered perspective reduces the emotional and cognitive load overall.

The hypothesis proved to be true in part, but only for men. Stress worsened the performance of men in three types of tasks. Why this occurs is unclear, although experts suspect the gender difference may be accounted for by the oxytocin system. Oxytocin is a hormone connected with social behaviors, and a previous study had found that during stressful conditions women had higher levels of oxytocin.[6] Focusing on relationships can be a superpower for women to leverage in trying times, combating stress and building resilience.

Building Resilience in Crisis Situations

Research has proven that, when companies experience a crisis, leaders must motivate employees and unite them around a clear direction, precise objectives, and an inspirational vision.[7] I certainly found this to be true when I first took the leadership reins at Performics. There were a multitude of problems that needed to be addressed—from a shortage of new clients, to existing client attrition, to accounts receivable...the list went on.

I could have easily dedicated 100 percent of my time and energy to fixing practical business problems. That approach certainly would not have been unique. In fact, the prior leader had acknowledged many of these issues and had been actively working to solve them, with little success.

I chose to focus on the so-called "soft" issues and value them as equally important to the many other product, process, and structural issues affecting the business. I sensed that the organization as a whole was "bruised" emotionally and the culture was suffering. I sensed that, while focusing entirely on the practical issues certainly would have solved important problems, without an intrinsic commitment from the team, our efforts around the "harder" issues would not produce long-term results.

My instinctual focus turned out to be the right decision, and spending time and dollars focused on teamwork and inspiration, and even individual motivation, created valuable positive momentum. It also created team resilience that sustained our positive momentum when it took longer and required more effort than anticipated to turn new business around. Without this relationship and collaborative focus, the setbacks we experienced could have caused people to lose trust. Investing in relationships and people can be perceived as a "nice to have" asset, but, in my experience, it is a necessity.

Creating Organizational Resilience Through Transformational Leadership

A relationship focus can translate into organizational benefits as well. Research has shown that leaders who use the transformational leadership style can help an organization be more resilient. Women leaders are more predisposed to focus on the welfare of others during stressful situations. This has obvious benefits for overall organizational morale. Research indicates that behaviors associated with the Grace perspective can have a positive and statistically significant effect on perceived organizational resiliency.[8]

One study found that leaders who were trained in transformational leadership created more team resiliency.[9] This study was built on the Grace approach to leadership and the idea of leadership being shared among all team members, as opposed to vertical leadership, or leadership placed on one position in the team. Researchers measured decreased team performance and recovery, and found that transformational-trained teams recovered faster than those using a transactional approach and showed greater overall resilience. The key distinguishing factor contributing to resilience was collaboration.

Collaboration: Key to Organizational Resilience

Transformational leaders create environments where individuals feel supported, valued, and appreciated. Collaboration is especially important as organizations become more cross-functional and information is held at every level. Being able to access information quickly and easily and disseminate it throughout the organization during a time of crisis is vital. Yet, collaborative work is not easy.

A study published in *Harvard Business Review* found that a mere 3 to 5 percent of employees drive the majority of collaborative work across organizations, and the lion's share of that collaborative work tends to fall on women.[10] This is because women are more focused on relationships and therefore more likely to assist others. With their skills in collaboration, empathy, and a focus on relationships, women can bring higher job satisfaction to individuals and teams. Inspiring, driven, decisive, confident, and powerful leaders are resilient leaders, and resilient leaders build resilient organizations.

In summary, having resilience is about the ability to bounce back, cope, renew, and revitalize when faced with challenges. Transformative leaders are positive, focused, and yet flexible—skills that enable them to thrive in the disruptive, fast-paced change occurring in today's workplace environments. Leaders possessing resilience demonstrate the four foundational behaviors: confidence, accountability, collaboration, and initiative. Collaboration is a key ingredient in Grace's relationship-focused style of leadership. Confidence, accountability, and initiative are consistent with the traditional Grit style of leadership. The magic formula to building resilience is to combine the qualities of Grace with Grit. This combination will build resilience for people, teams, and organizations to keep them moving forward in the face of challenge.

Historical Inspiration:
Pauline Bayer

Resilience against all odds

For the women who settled and lived in Wyoming during the early 1900s, resilience was fundamental, not only individually but for their entire families. The harsh climate and untamed wilderness presented never-ending challenges. Women who thrived in these unpredictable conditions also had families who prospered.

One such woman was Pauline Bayer, who became one of Wyoming's first women mail carriers. Her mail route was considered to be one of the worst in Wyoming, if not the most perilous in all of the Western United States, running more than one hundred miles through the mountains of the Continental Divide from cities known today as Pinedale to South Pass City.[11] According to a book titled *Wyoming Pioneer Women*, written by her family, the high elevation (over 7,000 feet) on the route meant winter persisted from September through June in a mix of mountain and high desert terrain. The trail was tough for a team of horses pulling a wagon laden with mail, even in the best of weather conditions.

In the winter, Pauline drove a horse-drawn toboggan and snuggled under blankets with a foot-warming hot brick or stray cat or dog that she was known for picking up along the route. Often portions of the route could not be accessed using horses during the winter and sometimes Pauline had to resort to skis or snowshoes to get the mail into the hands of its recipient.

Pauline Bayer and her husband, Albert Bayer, were awarded the route in 1906 as the low bidders in the government auction. They realized relatively quickly that the route would be tougher than they had anticipated but decided to honor the contract anyway. They struggled to retain subcontracted drivers over portions of the route, so Pauline took over a good portion of the route herself.

Forty years old when she took on the mail-carrier job, Pauline Bayer had spent her life before that giving to others and tackling any obstacle that came her way. She had served as an untrained doctor to sick neighbors, and even acted as a midwife to assist births in nearby communities where there were no doctors. She had an uncanny sense of direction and rescued other drivers who lost their way in blizzards on more than one occasion. She delivered the mail for twelve consecutive years.

Nothing deterred Pauline's gritty spirit. She encountered tough situations with creativity, including wearing a bonnet, in the style of Martha Washington, but which she had adapted for her needs, using zinc instead of cloth for the brim to protect her face and eyes from the harsh elements she encountered on the mail routes, when her dark glasses weren't enough. As Al Kolman wrote in the afterword of the book *Wyoming Pioneer Woman*, Bayer lived by the motto of "put your shoulder to the wheel and carry your own load." He described her as someone who "never ran from adversity, in fact, she walked through the middle of everything that ever challenged her." She lived with resilience until the day she died on June 27, 1944, at seventy-eight years old.

Quick Reference Guide

Resilience

The ability to bounce back, cope, renew, and revitalize when faced with challenges

If you bring the Grace perspective:

- Tap into your innate resilience—you have it...you were born with it!
- Leverage the power of relationships, collaborating and supporting others.
- Remember that collaboration is a powerful differentiator and, combined with confidence, accountability, and initiative, is the key to building and sustaining organizational resilience.
- Remember that transformational leaders believe their followers can perform, which empowers and inspires the group, also creating organizational resilience.

- Don't allow setbacks to affect other leadership behaviors, such as confidence, drive, decision making, or embracing power.
- Replenish and refuel yourself so that you can fill others.

If you bring the Grit perspective:

- Be aware of the tendency to work in isolation and become ego-centric under stress, and combat this by reaching out to team members, listening, and making time for exercise, sleep, and other stress-relieving activities.
- Leverage collaborators in the organization to fill gaps, if required.
- Maintain an empathetic and relationship-focused team approach.
- Remember that reaching out and collaborating with others can be a strength, not a weakness, and, through collaboration, work to build individual and organizational resilience.

Conclusion

I first met Robin in 2005 when I was working for Hewlett-Packard and Google assigned her to work on the HP account. Robin was the human face of Google: smart, warm, kind, honest, trustworthy, sincere, responsive, authentic, real. I was lucky to work with her for a number of years, first as a client and then as a partner when I joined Moxie and Performics.

Through it all, our relationship grew and we became close friends. Both of the businesses we worked for benefited from our relationship. One of my proudest achievements of our combined efforts was cocreating the first-ever short-film competition created by participants on YouTube, shortly after the company was acquired by Google. It was called HP: ProjectDirect. The competition was an industry first, with incredible results, but most important to me was the experience of uniting individuals who worked for different, sometimes competing, organizations into a unified team aligned around an inspirational goal.

Robin did not view herself as an extraordinary leader; she was modest and at times lacked confidence, and she had an ambivalent relationship with power. However, I knew her as a remarkable, courageous transformational leader who touched many people. Robin blended Grace with Grit beautifully by genuinely caring for people first.

In a world where many leaders believe that having a focus on people will compromise their work, this amazing woman proved that there is no need to choose power instead of people. She did not have the traditional leadership presence of Grit. Robin was subtler, and her power was that she led through others. Yet, she was respected, admired, and delivered results, adapting to Google's changing business needs, from its early start-up days to the modern, sophisticated media landscape.

The business evolved, but Robin's leadership approach stayed constant. She is a shining example to me of being good at both the "hard" and "soft" sides of leadership. I think we are better at both by not compromising *either*.

Four years ago, Robin passed away suddenly following complications from minor surgery. She was young, too young to leave behind a husband and three young daughters. She had accomplished much in life, and should have had years of opportunities ahead of her. When I was asked by her husband to speak at her memorial, I was honored and overwhelmed. I didn't know how I could even begin to communicate publicly what she had meant to me, let alone capture what she meant to the world she touched.

So, I began collecting the hundreds of comments and posts on social media sites and fed them into a word-cloud generator (a visual representation of a grouping of words in different font sizes, as to show relative frequency). The words represented in the word cloud were extraordinarily inspiring: leader, friend, mentor, passionate, fun, warm, laugh, love, energy, and—most predictably—family and smile. It's a moving collection of words that I have printed out and keep posted above my desk to inspire me each and every day.

Robin Tag Cloud

Robin was not just an inspiration to women; she also had a profound impact on men who worked for and with her. What she did best was advocating for and equally valuing people first. In reading hundreds of messages from her colleagues, and interviewing a number of individuals after her passing, I learned that Robin started every conversation by asking about a person's home life first. Because of this small gesture, she made each individual feel as though they could bring their entire self to work. She demonstrated that it is safe to have life conversations at work.

This sounds really simple and rather obvious, and maybe even a bit ludicrous. Obviously, life conversations should be safe at work! But this is not obvious to most leaders. Despite the advances in work–life balance, men in particular are not comfortable in bringing their entire selves to work.

Bringing Our Whole Selves to Work

In talking with dozens of men about whether they feel comfortable telling their boss they are headed out for a child's doctor appointment versus a personal doctor appointment, the majority of them said they would rather tell their boss they are leaving the office for a haircut instead of a domestic task.

During a presentation in San Francisco, one young woman raised her hand and said, "I don't understand—why is it important for men to feel OK bringing their whole selves to work?" Before I could even respond, a man in the audience raised his hand and asked if he could answer the question.

"Because I carry this weight around every day," he said. "I don't feel comfortable talking about my home life, and yet my family is a big part of my life. I want to feel free to talk about my whole life."

Concern About Backlash

According to the latest survey published by the White House Council of Economic Advisers, 77 percent of workers reported having some ability to take a form of unpaid leave. Nearly three-quarters have access to take unpaid leave if they have an illness, and 60 percent can do so for the birth of a child. But even when family leave is available, men may forego it because they cannot afford lost wages or they fear negative consequences.

The LeanIn.org and McKinsey study also found evidence that employees (both men and women) are reluctant to participate in flexible employee work programs for fear of being penalized. More than 90 percent of both women and men reported they believed taking extended family leave would hurt their position at work, and more than half believed it would hurt them a great deal.

Balancing Career and Home Life

Women are also far more likely than men to take a leave from their career to raise families, pursue education, support elder family members, or pursue other interests. Unfortunately, this often places them at a disadvantage when pursuing senior leadership and management positions. Companies often still abide by the dictates of a traditional linear career model, even though it's no longer relevant. To take advantage of the best and brightest talent, new dynamic models should be adopted so individuals who choose to take a leave of absence can resume their place on the career ladder later.

When it comes to managing workplace perceptions around work and home, men face their own set of challenges. The Bureau of Labor Statistics' "American Time Use Survey" documented an increase in the number of hours men are spending on both childcare and domestic labor.[1] The research suggested that men want to be more involved in their families, play a larger role in child care and household responsibilities, and support their partners in their career pursuits. However, the traditional leadership standard, with its hierarchical model of leadership, rewards time served and "anytime, anywhere" availability. This likely has an impact on whether or not men play a more active role in home and family activities, because the stereotype affects them more.

Developing Centered Leadership

As a coach, I spend time advising leaders about the importance of leveraging their innate strengths. There is power in leading from an authentic self. Sometimes this is difficult for leaders to do based on their individual style and how this style matches with their work environment. If there is a mismatch, it often requires the leader to truly question whether the current role or company is right for her. Leaders are better if they can truly be their authentic selves. This requires driving from a center of strength rather than relying on others' standards. I call this "centered leadership."

Paving the Path to Leadership

Paving the path to leadership is more complicated than just understanding gender differences. For women, leadership behaviors are often more complicated than for men because these behaviors are interwoven with other concepts, especially power and confidence, that are vital to leadership success but about which women feel ambivalent. The love-hate relationship women have with these behaviors is fascinating, frustrating, and enlightening at the same time. My research has indicated that, even if women understand the behavior differences between themselves and their male counterparts and use their innate ability to lead in a transformative manner, they must still embrace power and confidence to truly be successful in rising through the ranks of leadership. However, their view of power and confidence may not fit the stereotype.

Now is the time for companies and leaders to embrace a new approach to leadership, one that can empower the next generation of remarkable and courageous women. To do this, we will need to challenge the traditional command-and-control leadership styles of the past and instead adopt the progressive, transformational leadership style for the future. While evidence is growing regarding the overwhelming benefits of transformational leadership for organizations, barriers persist.

Challenging these barriers will require courage, listening, discussing, and learning from one another in a way we never have before. Using the blueprint of transformational leadership can help guide organizations and individuals alike. Anyone can become a transformational leader. The transformational leadership style is androgynous, meaning it incorporates both masculine and feminine behaviors. This is where Grace meets Grit. Women and men can both use this leadership style to become remarkable, courageous leaders. This mixing of masculine and feminine strengths will create the next generation of inspiring, driven, decisive, confident, powerful, resilient, and centered leaders.

To truly embrace transformational leadership, we must reframe how leadership is defined in most organizations today. It is my hope that *Grace Meets Grit* helps to facilitate these conversations—now, today, in everyday interactions. The language of *Grace Meets Grit* can help to remove the contention that sometimes arises when it becomes an accusatory "men do this" and "women do that" discussion. It can also shine a light on the value of having diverse styles in leadership situations.

Young women often ask for my guidance in pursuing a leadership role. This is how this book came about, and I would offer the four points of advice below to every woman seeking leadership opportunities.

Expect to Confront the Traditional Leadership Style

First, I would encourage you to go in with your eyes open. Understand that there will be challenges and prepare for them. Assuming that men and women think the same and that gender-based misunderstandings are a thing of the past will cause frustration and disillusionment. Come to grips with the fact that, despite all of the advancements made in accepting diverse styles, the leadership standard is still largely biased toward the traditional male style. Learn about this style, but don't assume that adopting it is the key to rising through the ranks. Don't be afraid to challenge the status quo, ask why, and offer alternatives. If it appears you are being judged unfairly, say so.

Hang on to Your Superpower

Second, recognize that you possess an innate secret power in your inherent relationship-focused approach to leadership. No matter what pressures you experience or how uncomfortable the environment becomes, remember that this skill is valuable. It will help you to inspire followers and obtain quantum results because you can leverage the power of the whole organization and make better, more-informed decisions. As business becomes increasingly global and cross-functional, and sharing information even more critical, teamwork will be seen as increasingly important to organizational success. The skill of building and maintaining relationships will become progressively valuable. You own it—use it, value it.

Embrace Power and Confidence

Third, to obtain more senior-level positions, women must be powerful and confident, and be comfortable owning these leadership behaviors. We will not see an increase of women in key roles until women exercise their inner Grit and embrace power and confidence as key behaviors leading to success. This means they must practice acting powerful and confident and prioritize developing these behaviors and other leadership competencies.

Find Your Center

Finally, let go of being perfect and trying to keep every aspect of life in balanced harmony. Instead, work on developing a sense of center—or placing yourself at the core instead of evenly distributing it across segments of life. Having a strong sense of center will also help you develop confidence and personal power. Being centered also means supporting other women, at all levels, and other men in bringing their entire selves to work.

If we accomplish this, we will accomplish much. There will be less discomfort, more collaboration, better places to work, and greater company value by embracing both Grace and Grit qualities. Both men and women must work together to create a new paradigm. It is my hope that through *Grace Meets Grit* women will bring their real, transparent, honest, and authentic selves to work and be recognized, valued, and appreciated for their unique leadership contributions.

Acknowledgments

This book would not be in your hands today without the support and contribution of so many individuals who helped bring it to life. Writing *Grace Meets Grit* was a very personal experience for me. I wanted it to be intimate, because I heard from so many individuals that this was a very personal, complex subject, where behaviors are subtle and nuanced and work life and home life are intertwined into issues with many layers. Through my own personal experiences, encouraged by the voices of many others, the message came through loud and clear how important it is to begin the next level of the gender conversation, and that bias awareness and gender equality are not enough. I hope that this book will fulfill that promise and bring to life new conversations that will drive lasting behavior changes in the workplace.

I want to begin by thanking the many women and men who were brave enough to share with me their personal stories, and even feelings, about their experiences in work situations that are sometimes sensitive. Many did not want me to reveal names but provided color, validated or clarified ideas, and helped me bring to life leadership behaviors in an authentic and relevant way. Others came to me and volunteered their own stories after public presentations I gave and provided words of encouragement about the importance of the message in this book. I want to thank these individuals—you know who you are.

A thank-you also to the amazing Lauren Wood, PhD, now at Yahoo, who helped to quantify the data around the Grace and Grit behaviors. The questionnaires would not have been possible without her analysis, support, and dedication to ensure the research was statistically viable and accurate. She was also invaluable in accessing other critical research studies referenced in this book.

To the amazing, passionate, and talented Dell Larcen, thank you for providing me with the opportunity to learn from the best and become an inspirational leadership coach. I can only hope to someday have the industry reputation, elegance, thoughtfulness, and insight that you do.

Mom, thank you for helping me to organize three chapters that were awkward in flow and for the continual inspiration in life. As my very first editor (when I was only fourteen) who helped me understand the writing process, you are, and always will be, the voice driving me on in my head.

To my partner, champion, and best friend, Rob, thank you for always being by my side with dedication, devotion, and love. Writing a book while working full time and managing the million other demands in life can take a toll on a relationship but, because of your patience and commitment, ours never wavered.

To Mesa and Kenyon, thank you for trusting me to put down in words and share for the first time the painful story in which we all played a part.

Thanks to the amazing Cindy Gallop, Laura Kofoid, and Wenda Millard for sharing your own stories. You are all Grace meets Grit. To Sally Hogshead, whom I admire in so many ways, thank you for providing me with constant encouragement for both of my books. I aspire to be all that you have become.

A heartfelt thank-you goes to the amazing Amy Jameson, who helped me smooth out the final rough edges in the manuscript. You immediately grasped the spirit of *Grace Meets Grit* and guided the final product to an entirely new level.

Finally, a huge nod to the wonderful Bibliomotion team, particularly Erika and Alicia, but the entire, talented team. Without your contributions and encouragement, *Grace Meets Grit* would not be what it is today. Bibliomotion has been a true dream-team partner.

Notes

Chapter 1

1. Alexandra Kaley, Erin Kelly, and Frank Dobbin, "Best Practices or Best Guesses? Assessing the Efficacy of Corporate Affirmative Action and Diversity Policies," *American Sociological Review* 71 (2006): 589–617.

Chapter 2

1. Bob Sherwin, "Why Women Are More Effective Leaders Than Men," *Business Insider*, January 24, 2014, http://www.businessinsider.com/study-women-are-better-leaders-2014-1.
2. Pavle Sabec, *How Times Have Changed? CEO Gender Gap Analysis of the S&P 500*, S&P Capital IQ, November 2015.
3. Catalyst, *2013 Catalyst Census: Fortune 500 Women Executive Officers and Top Earners*, 2013, http://www.catalyst.org/knowledge/2013-catalyst-census-fortune-500-women-executive-officers-and-top-earners.
4. LeanIn.org and McKinsey & Company, *Women in the Workplace*, 2015.
5. Joanna Barsh and Larelina Yee, *Special Report: Unlocking the Full Potential of Women in the U.S. Economy*, McKinsey & Company, April 2012.
6. Caliper, *Women Leaders*, December 2014, 10–14.
7. Barsh and Yee, *Unlocking the Full Potential of Women,* 17–19.
8. Academy of Management Learning & Education, *Taking Gender into Account: Theory and Design for Women's Leadership Development Programs*, September 2011.
9. Hermina Ibarra, Robin J. Ely, and Deborah M. Kolb, "Women Rising: The Unseen Barriers," *Harvard Business Review*, September 2013, 68–76.
10. LeanIn.org and McKinsey, *Women in the Workplace*.

11. Kathy Caprino, *Breakthrough: The Professional Woman's Guide to Claiming a Life of Passion, Power, and Purpose* (San Francisco: Berrett-Koehler Publishers, 2008), 26–44, 98–101.

12. Alexandra Kalev, Erin Kelly, and Frank Dobbin, "Best Practices or Best Guesses? Assessing the Efficacy of Corporate Affirmative Action and Diversity Policies," *American Sociological Review* 71 (2006): 601.

13. Kalev, Kelly, and Dobbin, "Best Practices or Best Guesses?," 592.

14. Deborah Tannen, *You Just Don't Understand* (New York: Morrow Publishing, 1990), 13.

15. Theodore Satterthwaite et al., "Linked Sex Differences in Cognition and Functional Connectivity in Youth," *Cerebral Cortex,* March 18, 2014.

16. Linda Lee-Eling, Ric Marshall, Damion Rallis, and Matt Moscardi, *Women on Boards: Global Trends in Gender Diversity on Corporate Boards*, MSCI ESG Research, Inc., November 2015.

17. Credit Suisse, *The CS Gender 3000: Women in Senior Management*, September 2014, 5.

18. LeanIn.org and McKinsey, *Women in the Workplace.*

19. Bob Sherwin, "Why Women Are More Effective Leaders Than Men," *Business Insider*, January 24, 2014, http://www.businessinsider.com/study-women-are -better-leaders-2014-1.

20. McKinsey Global Institute, *The Power of Parity: How Advancing Women's Equality Can Add $12 Trillion to Global Growth*, September 2015.

21. Claartje Vinkenburg, Marloes L. van Engen, Alice H. Eagly, and Mary C. Johannesen-Schmidt, "An Exploration in Stereotypical Beliefs About Leadership Styles: Is Transformational Leadership a Route to Women's Promotion?" *The Leadership Quarterly* 22 (2011): 10–12.

22. Pew Research Center, *Women and Leadership: Public Says Women Are Equally Qualified, but Barriers Persist*, January 2015, http://www.pewsocialtrends. org/2015/01/14/women-and-leadership.

23. Rob Cross, Reb Rebele, and Adam Grant, "Collaborative Overload," *Harvard Business Review*, January/February 2016: 57–60.

24. Li Ning et al., "Achieving More with Less: Extra Milers' Behavioral Influences in Crews," *Journal of Applied Psychology* 100 (2015): 1031–1037.

Chapter 3

1. Robert R. Blake and Anne A. McCanse, *Leadership Dilemmas—Grid Solutions* (Houston, TX: Gulf Publishing Company, 1991), 44–77.

2. Jeanine L. Prime and Nancy M. Carter, "Women 'Take Care,' Men 'Take Charge': Managers' Stereotypic Perceptions of Women and Men Leaders," *The Psychologist-Manager Journal* 12 (2009): 25–49.

3. Prime and Carter, "Women 'Take Care,'" 34.

4. Bob Sherwin, "Why Women Are More Effective Leaders Than Men," *Business Insider,* January 24, 2014, http://www.businessinsider.com/study-women-are-better-leaders-2014-1.

5. Deborah Tannen, *You Just Don't Understand* (New York: Morrow Publishing, 1990), 13.

6. Dan Martin, "Do Women or Men Make the Best Leaders?," Business Zone, June 27, 2012, http://www.businesszone.co.uk/decide/scale/do-men-or-women-make-the-best-leaders.

7. Management Research Group, *Gender Differences and Leadership*, 2013.

8. Pew Research Center, *Women and Leadership: Public Says Women Are Equally Qualified, but Barriers Persist,* January 2015, http://www.pewsocialtrends.org/2015/01/14/women-and-leadership.

9. Caliper, *Women Leaders*, December 2014, 7.

10. Andrea Lai, "Transformational-Transactional Leadership Theory," 2011 AHS Capstone Projects, Paper 17, http://digitalcommons.olin.edu/ahs_capstone_2011/17.

11. R. B. Kaiser, "Leadership and the Fate of Organizations," *American Psychologist* 63 (2008): 96–110, 99.

12. B. M. Bass, *Leadership and Performance Beyond Expectations* (New York: Free Press, 1985).

13. G. Wang, "Transformational Leadership and Performance Across Criteria and Levels: A Meta-Analytics Review of 25 Years of Research," *Group and Organization Management* 36 (2011): 233–270.

14. James MacGregor Burns, *Transforming Leadership* (New York: Grove Press, 2003).

15. Lai, "Transformational-Transactional Leadership Theory."

16. *Hewlett-Packard Employee* Handbook, obtained at new employee orientation, April 1992.

17. A. H. Eagly, and L. L. Carli, "The Female Leadership Advantage: An Evaluation of the Evidence," *The Leadership Quarterly* 14 (2003): 807–834, 821.

18. Alice H. Eagly, Mary C. Johannesen-Schmidt, and Marloes L. van Engan, "Transformational, Transactional and Lassez-Faire Leadership Styles," *Psychological Bulletin* 129 (2003): 569–591, doi: 10.1037/0033-2909.129.4.569.

19. Claartje J. Vinkenburg, Marloes L. van Engan, Alice H. Eagly, and Mary C. Johannesen-Schmidt, "An Exploration of Stereotypical Beliefs About Leadership

Styles: Is Transformational Leadership a Route to Women's Promotion?," *The Leadership Quarterly* 22 (2011): 10–21.

20. Millennials Intelligence Group Study, *Columbus Dispatch*, March 30, 2014.

21. Laura Vanderkam, "The New Meaning of Workplace Mentorship," *Fast Company*, January 10, 2016, http://www.fastcompany.com/3040938/the-new -meaning-of-workplace-mentorship.

22. Kathy Caprino, "How Much Has Our Perception of Great Leadership Shifted Over the Past Decade and What Has Changed?" Forbes.com, August 29, 2015, http://www.forbes.com/sites/kathycaprino/2015/08/29/how-much-has-our -perception-of-great-leadership-shifted-over-the-past-decade-and-what-has -changed/#49ad1b87538e.

Chapter 4

1. Jack Zenger and Joseph Folkman, "What Inspiring Leaders Do," *Harvard Business Review*, June 20, 2013.

2. Jeanine L. Prime and Nancy M. Carter, "Women 'Take Care,' Men 'Take Charge': Managers' Stereotypic Perceptions of Women and Men Leaders," *The Psychologist-Manager Journal* 12 (2009): 25–49, 44.

3. John H. Zenger and Joseph R. Folkman, *The Extraordinary Leader: Turning Good Managers into Great Leaders* (New York: McGraw Hill, 2009).

4. *2011 HOW Report*, LRN Corp, *Chief Learning Officer*, http://howmetrics.lrn.com.

5. Aaron De Smet, Rodgers Palmer, and William Schaninger, *The Missing Link: Connecting Organizational and Financial Performance*, McKinsey & Company, 2007.

6. David C. Forman and Friso van der Oord, "The Eight Principles of Inspirational Leadership," Talent Management, February 21, 2013, http://www.talentmgt .com/articles/eight-principles-of-inspirational-leadership.

7. Madhura Ingalhalikara et al., "Sex Differences in the Structural Connectome of the Human Brain," *Proceedings of the National Academy of Sciences* 11 (2013): 823–828, doi: 10.1073/pnas.1316909110.

8. Institute of Leadership & Management (ILM) and Management Today, *Index of Leadership Trust 2010*, ILM, September 2010, https://www.i-l-m.com/-/media/ ILM%20Website/Documents/Information%20for%20centres/ILM_Index _Leadership_Trust_2010_Report%20pdf.ashx.

9. Chantal Free, Carole Hathaway, Nick Lynn, and Angela Paul, "Looking After the Number Ones: Strategies for Engaging and Retaining Top Talent," Towers Watson, *HR Matters*, February 2015, https://www.towerswatson.com/en-GB/ Insights/Newsletters/Europe/HR-matters/2015/02/HR-Matters-February-2015.

10. *Merriam-Webster Dictionary,* 6th ed., s.v. "transparent."

11. Ketchum Inc., "2014 Ketchum Leadership Communication Monitor (KLCM)," May 2014, https://www.ketchum.com/leadership-communication-monitor-2014.

12. Michelle K. Ryan, S. Alexander Haslam, Mette D. Hersby, and Renata Bongiorno, "Think Crisis—Think Female. The Glass Cliff and Contextual Variation in the Think Manager—Think Male Stereotype," *Journal of Applied Psychology* 96 (2011): 470–484.

13. Shane Schutte, "Female CEOs: Business Turnaround Extraordinaires?," Real Business, October 28, 1013, http://realbusiness.co.uk/article/28252-female-ceos-business-turnaround-extraordinaires.

14. Chris Bart and Gregory McQueen, "Why Women Make Better Directors," *International Journal of Business Governance and Ethics* 8 (2013): 93, doi: 10.1504/IJBGE.2013.052743.

15. Teva J. Scheer, *Governor Lady: The Life and Times of Nellie Tayloe Ross*, Missouri Biography Series (Columbia, MO: University of Missouri Press, 2005), 170, 176.

Chapter 5

1. Kevin Kruse, "What Is Leadership?" Forbes.com, April 9, 2013, http://www.forbes.com/sites/kevinkruse/2013/04/09/what-is-leadership/#1a5bddae713e.

2. Matthew Lieberman, "Should Leaders Focus on Results, or on People?" *Harvard Business Review*, December 27, 2013, http://blogs.hbr.org/2013/12/should-leaders-focus-on-results-or-on-people.

3. Matthew D. Lieberman, *Social: Why Our Brains Are Wired To Connect* (Oxford: Oxford University Press, 2013), 384.

4. Caliper, *Women Leaders,* December 2014, 6.

5. Jack Zenger and Joseph Folkman, "Are Women Better Leaders Than Men?," *Harvard Business Review*, March 15, 2012, https://hbr.org/2012/03/a-study-in-leadership-women-do/.

6. Barsh and Yee, *Unlocking the Full Potential of Women,* McKinsey & Company, 2012, 7.

7. Lawrence A. Pfaff & Associates, "Perceptions of Women and Men Leaders Following 360-Degree Feedback Evaluations," *Performance Improvement Quarterly* 26 (2013), first published online April 17, 2013, 39.

8. K. J. Boatwright and L. Forrest, "Leadership Preferences: The Influence of Gender and Needs for Connection on Workers' Ideal Preferences for Leadership Behaviors, *The Journal of Leadership & Organizational Studies* 7 (2000): 18–34, 28–31, doi: 10.1177/107179190000700202.

Chapter 6

1. Jeanine L. Prime and Nancy M. Carter, "Women 'Take Care,' Men 'Take Charge': Managers' Stereotypic Perceptions of Women and Men Leaders," *The Psychologist-Manager Journal* 12 (2009): 25.

2. Prime and Carter, "Women 'Take Care,'" 25.

3. L. Tomova et al., "Is Stress Affecting Our Ability to Tune into Others? Evidence for Gender Differences in the Effects of Stress on Self-Other Distinction," *Psychoneuroendrocrinology* 43 (2014): 95–104.

4. G. Domes et al. "Oxytocin Improves Mind-Reading in Humans," *Biological Psychiatry* 61 (2007), 731–733.

5. R. Hurlemann et al., "Oxytocin Enhances Amygdala-Dependent, Socially Reinforced Learning and Emotional Empathy in Humans," *Journal of Neuroscience* 30 (2010): 859–866, 862–863.

6. V. Colonnello, F. S. Chen, J. Panksepp, and M. Heinrichs, "Oxytocin Sharpens Self-Other Perceptual Boundary," *Psychoneuroendocrinology* 38 (2013): 2996–3002.

7. University of California, Irvine, "Intelligence in Men and Women Is a Gray and White Matter," Science Daily, January 22, 2005, https://www.sciencedaily.com/releases/2005/01/050121100142.htm.

8. Cathy Benko and Bill Pelster, "How Women Decide," *Harvard Business Review*, September 2013, https://hbr.org/2013/09/how-women-decide.

9. Chris Bart and Gregory McQueen, "Why Women Make Better Directors," *International Journal of Business Governance and Ethics* 8, no. 1 (2013): 93, doi: 10.1504/IJBGE.2013.052743; "Women Make Better Decisions Than Men," *International Journal of Business Governance and Ethics* (2015).

10. Rana Rashid Rehman and Ajmal Wahee, "Transformational Leadership Style As a Predictor of Decision Making Styles: Moderating Role of Emotional Intelligence," *Pakistan Journal of Commerce and Social Sciences* 6 (2012): 257–268, 262.

Chapter 7

1. Deborah Tannen, "The Power of Talk: Who Gets Heard and Why," *Harvard Business Review*, September/October 1995, https://hbr.org/1995/09/the-power-of-talk-who-gets-heard-and-why.

2. Katty Kay and Claire Shipman, *The Confidence Code: The Science and Art of Self-Assurance—What Women Should Know* (New York: HarperCollins, 2014), 220–241.

3. Katty Kay and Claire Shipman, "The Confidence Gap," *The Atlantic*, May 2014, http://www.theatlantic.com/magazine/archive/2014/05/the-confidence-gap/359815/.

4. Kay and Shipman, "The Confidence Gap."

5. Kay and Shipman, "The Confidence Gap."

6. Ernesto Reuben, Pedro Rey-Biel, Paola Sapienza, and Luigi Zingales, "The Emergence of Male Leadership in Competitive Environments," IZA, Discussion Paper No. 5300 November 2010. http://ftp.iza.org/dp5300.pdf.

7. U. Gneezy and A. Rustichini, "Gender and Competition at a Young Age," *American Economic Review* 94 (2004): 377–381, 379-381; and U. Gneezy, M. Niederle, and A. Rustichini, "Performance in Competitive Environments: Gender Differences," *Quarterly Journal of Economics* 118 (2003): 1049–1074, 1057–1061.

8. ILM, *Ambition and Gender at Work*, 2011, 3.

9. Grace Killelea, *The Confidence Effect: Every Woman's Guide to the Attitude That Attracts Success*, American Management Association, 2016, chapter 3.

10. Cameron Anderson, Sebastian Brion, Don A. Moore, and Jessica A. Kennedy, "A Status-Enhancement Account of Overconfidence," *Journal of Personality and Social Psychology* 103 (2009): 718–735, 722–727, doi: http://dx.doi.org/10.1037/a0029395.

11. Kay and Shipman, "The Confidence Gap," 44.

12. Carol S. Dweck, *Mindset: The New Psychology of Success* (New York: Random House, 2006), 32.

13. T. A. Larson, *History of Wyoming* (Lincoln: University of Nebraska Press, 1979), 69.

14. Boyd Papers, Wyoming State Archives, Cheyenne, WPA File #584, Stephen Boyd obituary, "Laramie Republican," Oct. 16, 1917, http://uwacadweb.uwyo.edu/RobertsHistory/Readings_chapter_4.htm

33. Records from Jackson Hole Historical Society.

Chapter 8

1. Paul H. Hersey, Kenneth H. Blanchard and Dewey E. Johnson, *Management of Organizational Behavior*, 10th ed. (Englewood Cliffs, NJ: Prentice-Hall, 2012), 127.

2. Anne Perschel and Jane Perdue, "Women and the Paradox of Power: 8 Keys for Transforming Business Culture." Women 2.0., January 2012, http://women2.com/2012/09/14/women-and-the-paradox-of-power-8-keys-for-transforming-business-culture/.

3. Pew Research Center, *Women and Leadership: Public Says Women Are Equally Qualified, but Barriers Persist*, January 2015, http://www.pewsocialtrends .org/2015/01/14/women-and-leadership, 16.

4. Deborah Tannen, *You Just Don't Understand* (New York: Harper Collins, 2013), 43–77.

5. ILM, "Ambition and Gender at Work," 2011, 7.

6. Perschel and Perdue, "Women and the Paradox of Power."

7. Sylvia Ann Hewlett and Melinda Marshall, *Women Want Five Things*, Center for Talent Innovation, December 2014, 14–17. (The text quoted is based on a survey of college-educated women in white-collar professions in the U.S., the U.K., and Germany.)

8. Hewlett and Marshall, *Women Want Five Things*, 5.

9. Hewlett and Marshall, *Women Want Five Things*, 21–5.

10. Hewlett and Marshall, *Women Want Five Things*, 12.

11. Hewlett and Marshall, *Women Want Five Things*, 25–27.

12. Hewlett and Marshall, *Women Want Five Things*, 12.

13. Hewlett and Marshall, *Women Want Five Things*, 31–33.

14. Hewlett and Marshall, *Women Want Five Things*, 34–37.

15. Ariane Hegewisch, Emily Ellis, Heidi Hartmann, *The Gender Wage Gap: 2014: Earnings Differences by Race and Ethnicity*, Institute for Policy Research, March 2015, 1.

16. Center for Creative Leadership, *The Role of Power in Effective Leadership*, 2008, 2.

17. Perschel and Perdue, "Women and the Paradox of Power."

18. Alice H. Eagly and Mary C. Johannesen-Schmidt, "The Leadership Styles of Men and Women," *Journal of Social Issues* 57, no. 4 (Winter 2001): 781–797, 789–792.

19. James R. Detert and Ethan R. Burris, "Can Your Employees Really Speak Freely?" *Harvard Business Review*, January 18, 2016, https://hbr.org/2016/01/ can-your-employees-really-speak-freely.

20. Michelle Herbison, "Cindy Gallop on Disrupting Sex, Diversity, Shared Value and Change from the Bottom Up," *Marketing Magazine*, August 19, 2015.

21. Records from Jackson Hole Historical Society.

Chapter 9

1. N. Amano and E. Iseki, "Introduction: Pick's Disease and Frontotemporal Dementia," *Neuropathology* 19 (1999): 417–421, 421.

2. E. Allison and D. Reeves, *Renewal Coaching Field Guide: How Effective Leaders Sustain Meaningful Change* (San Francisco: Jossey-Bass, 2011), 121.

3. Steven Snyder, "Why Resilience Is So Hard," *Harvard Business Review*, November 6, 2013, https://hbr.org/2013/11/why-is-resilience-so-hard/.

4. Steven B. Morse, "Racial and Gender Differences in the Viability of Extremely Low Birth Weight Infants: A Population-Based Study," *Pediatrics* 117 (2006): 106–108.

5. John F. Allen, Jim McKenna, and Susan Dominey, "Degrees of Resilience: Profiling Psychological Resilience and Prospective Academic Achievement in University Inductees," *British Journal of Guidance & Counselling*, May 13, 2013, 9–25, 18.

6. L. Tomova et al., "Is stress Affecting Our Ability to Tune into Others? Evidence for Gender Differences in the Effects of Stress on Self-Other Distinction," *Psychoneuroendrocrinology* 43 (2014): 95–104, 99-101.

7. McKinsey & Company, *Women Matter 3: Women Leaders, a Competitive Edge in and After the Crisis*, April 2010, 10–12.

8. Jesus N. Valero, Kyujin Jung, and Simon A. Andrew, "Does Transformational Leadership Build Resilient Public and Nonprofit Organizations?" *Disaster Prevention and Management* 24 (2015): 4–20, 16–19.

9. David A. Molenaar, "The Influence of Transformational Leadership Training on Crew Resilience" (master's thesis, University of Twente, Enschede, June 24, 2010), http://essay.utwente.nl/60477/.

10. Rob Cross, Reb Rebele, and Adam Grant, "Collaborative Overload," *Harvard Business Review*, January/February 2016, 57–60.

11. Otis Carney and Margaret Canfield Bayer, *Wyoming Pioneer Woman: Pauline Krueger Bayer* (Rock Spring, WY: Kolman Woodkraft, 1998), 218–225, 258–268.

Conclusion

1. Bureau of Labor Statistics, "American Time Use Survey," http://www.bls.gov/tus/.

References

Academy of Management Learning & Education, *Taking Gender into Account: Theory and Design for Women's Leadership Development Programs*, September 2011.

Allen, John F., Jim McKenna, and Susan Dominey, "Degrees of Resilience: Profiling Psychological Resilience and Prospective Academic Achievement in University Inductees," *British Journal of Guidance & Counselling*, May 13, 2013, 9–25.

Allison, E., and D. Reeves, *Renewal Coaching Field Guide: How Effective Leaders Sustain Meaningful Change* (San Francisco: Jossey-Bass, 2011).

Amano, N., and E. Iseki, "Introduction: Pick's Disease and Frontotemporal Dementia," *Neuropathology* 19 (1999): 417–421.

Anderson, Cameron, Sebastian Brion, Don A. Moore, and Jessica A. Kennedy, "A Status-Enhancement Account of Overconfidence," *Journal of Personality and Social Psychology* 103 (2009): 718–735, 722–727, doi: http://dx.doi.org/10.1037/a0029395.

Annis, Barbara, and John Gray, *Work with Me: The 8 Blind Spots Between Men and Women in Business* (New York: Palgrave Macmillan, 2013).

Annis, Barbara, and Keith Merron, *Gender Intelligence: Breakthrough Strategies for Increasing Diversity and Improving Your Bottom Line* (New York: HarperCollins e-book, 2013).

Bargau, Marian Aurelian, "Types of Leader in Organisation," Joint International Conferences, Performance and Risks in the European Economy, 2012.

Barsh, Joanna, and Laralina Yee, *Special Report: Unlocking the Full Potential of Women in the U.S. Economy*, McKinsey & Company, April 2012.

Bart, Chris, and Gregory McQueen, "Why Women Make Better Directors," *International Journal of Business Governance and Ethics* 8, no. 1 (2013): 93, doi: 10.1504/IJBGE.2013.052743.

Bass, B. M., *Leadership and Performance Beyond Expectations* (New York: Free Press, 1985).

Bazigos, Michael, Chris Gagnon, and Bill Schaninger, "Leadership in Context," *McKinsey Quarterly*, January 2016.

Benko, Cathy, and Bill Pelster, "How Women Decide," *Harvard Business Review*, September 2013, https://hbr.org/2013/09/how-women-decide.

Blake, Robert R., and Anne A. McCanse, *Leadership Dilemmas—Grid Solutions* (Houston, TX: Gulf Publishing Company, 1991), 44–77.

Boatwright, K. J., and L. Forrest, "Leadership Preferences: The Influence of Gender and Needs for Connection on Workers' Ideal Preferences for Leadership Behaviors," *The Journal of Leadership & Organizational Studies* 7 (2000): 18–34, 28-31, doi: 10.1177/107179190000700202.

Boyd Papers, Wyoming State Archives, Cheyenne, WPA File #584, Stephen Boyd obituary, "Laramie Republican," Oct. 16, 1917, http://uwacadweb.uwyo.edu/Roberts History/Readings_chapter_4.html.

Brizendine, Louann, M.D., *The Female Brain* (New York: Morgan Road Books, 2006).

Bureau of Labor Statistics, Time Use Study, http://www.bls.gov/tus/.

Burns, James MacGregor, *Transforming Leadership* (New York: Grove Press, 2003).

Caliper, *Women Leaders*, December 2014, 10–14.

Caprino, Kathy, "How Much Has Our Perception of Great Leadership Shifted Over the Past Decade and What Has Changed?" Forbes.com, August 29, 2015, http://www.forbes.com/sites/kathycaprino/2015/08/29/how-much-has-our -perception-of-great-leadership-shifted-over-the-past-decade-and-what-has -changed/#49ad1b87538e.

Caprino, Kathy, *Breakthrough: The Professional Woman's Guide to Claiming a Life of Passion, Power, and Purpose* (San Francisco: Berrett-Koehler Publishers, 2008).

Carney, Otis, and Margaret Canfield Bayer, *Wyoming Pioneer Woman: Pauline Krueger Bayer* (Rock Spring, WY: Kolman Woodkraft, 1998).

Catalyst, *2013 Catalyst Census: Fortune 500 Women Executive Officers And Top Earners*, 2013, http://www.catalyst.org/knowledge/2013-catalyst-census-fortune-500 -women-executive-officers-and-top-earners.

Center for Creative Leadership, *The Role of Power in Effective Leadership*, 2008.

Center for Talent Innovation, http://www.talentinnovation.org/Research-and-Insights/index.cfm?sorter=Women#list.

Clinton Foundation and Bill and Melinda Gates Foundation, *Full Participation Report*, No Ceilings Full Participation Project, January 2015.

Colonnello, V., F. S. Chen, J. Panksepp, and M. Heinrichs, "Oxytocin Sharpens Self-Other Perceptual Boundary," *Psychoneuroendocrinology* 38 (2013): 2996–3002.

Council of Economic Advisers, *The Economics of Paid and Unpaid Leave*, June 2014.

Credit Suisse, *The CS Gender 3000: Women in Senior Management*, September 2014.

Credit Suisse, *The Management Power Line,* September 2014.

Cross, Rob, Reb Rebele, and Adam Grant, "Collaborative Overload," *Harvard Business Review*, January/February 2016.

Detert, James R., and Ethan R. Burris, "Can Your Employees Really Speak Freely?" *Harvard Business Review*, January 18, 2016, https://hbr.org/2016/01/can-your-employees-really-speak-freely.

De Smet, Aaron, Rogers Palmer, and William Schaninger, *The Missing Link: Connecting Organizational and Financial Performance*, McKinsey & Company, 2007.

Dobbs, Randy, *Transformational Leadership: A Blueprint for Real Organizational Change* (Marion, MI: Parkhurst Brothers, Inc., 2010).

Domes, G., et al., "Oxytocin Improves Mind-Reading in Humans," *Biological Psychiatry* 61 (2007): 731–733.

Dweck, Carol S., *Mindset: The New Psychology of Success* (New York: Random House, 2006).

Eagly, Alice H., and Linda L. Carli, "The Female Leadership Advantage: An Evaluation of the Evidence," *The Leadership Quarterly* 14 (2003): 807–834, 821.

Eagly, Alice H., and Mary C. Johannesen-Schmidt, "The Leadership Styles of Men and Women," *Journal of Social Issues* 57, no 4 (Winter 2001): 781–797.

Eagly, Alice H., Mary C. Johannesen-Schmidt, and Marloes L. van Engan, "Transformational, Transactional and Lassez-Faire Leadership Styles," *Psychological Bulletin* 129 (2003): 569–591, doi: 10.1037/0033-2909.129.4.569 2003.

Eling, Linda Lee, Ric Marshall, Damion Rallis, and Matt Moscardi, *Women on Boards: Global Trends in Gender Diversity on Corporate Boards*, MSCI ESG Research, Inc., November 2015.

Felt, Gloria, "Four Signs That We're Near a Turning Point for Women in Leadership," *Fast Company*, January 7, 2016.

Forman, David C., and Friso van der Oord, "The Eight Principles of Inspirational Leadership," Talent Management, February 21, 2013, http://www.talentmgt .com/articles/eight-principles-of-inspirational-leadership.

Free, Chantal, Carole Hathaway, Nick Lynn, and Angela Paul, "Looking After the Number Ones: Strategies for Engaging and Retaining Top Talent," Towers Watson, *HR Matters*, February 2015; https://www.towerswatson.com/en-GB/ Insights/Newsletters/Europe/HR-matters/2015/02/HR-Matters-February-2015.

Fuqua Jr., Harold E., Kay E. Payne, and Joseph P. Cangemi, "Leadership and the Effective Use of Power," *National Forum of Educational Administration and Supervision Journal,* Western Kentucky University, 2011.

Gates, Robert M., *A Passion for Leadership: Lessons on Change and Reform from Fifty Years of Public Service* (New York: Alfred A. Knopf, 2016).

Gino, Francesca, and Gary P. Pisano, Gary, "Why Leaders Don't Learn from Success," *Harvard Business Review*, April 2011, https://hbr.org/2011/04/why-leaders -dont-learn-from-success.

Gneezy, U., and A. Rustichini, "Gender and Competition at a Young Age," *American Economic Review* 94 (2004): 377–381, 379–381.

Gneezy, U., M. Niederle, and A. Rustichini, "Performance in Competitive Environments: Gender Differences," *Quarterly Journal of Economics* 118 (2003): 1049– 1074.

Goleman, Daniel, *Social Intelligence* (New York: Random House, 2006).

Hegewisch, Ariane, Emily Ellis, and Heidi Hartmann, *The Gender Wage Gap: 2014: Earnings Differences by Race and Ethnicity*, Institute for Policy Research, March 2015.

Hersey, Paul H., Kenneth H. Blanchard, and Dewey E. Johnson, Dewey, *Management of Organizational Behavior*, 10th ed. (Englewood Cliffs, NJ: Prentice Hall 2012).

Hewlett, Sylvia Ann, and Melinda Marshall, *Women Want Five Things*, Center for Talent Innovation, December 2014.

Hewlett-Packard Employee Handbook, 1993.

Hurlemann, R., et al., "Oxytocin Enhances Amygdala-Dependent, Socially Reinforced Learning and Emotional Empathy in Humans," *Journal of Neuroscience* 30 (2010): 859–866.

Ibarra, Hermina, Robin J. Ely, Deborah M. Kolb, "Women Rising: The Unseen Barriers," *Harvard Business Review*, September 2013, 68–76.

Ingalhalikara, Madhura et al., "Sex Differences in the Structural Connectome of the Human Brain," *Proceedings of the National Academy of Sciences* 11 (2013): 823–828, doi: 10.1073/pnas.1316909110.

Institute of Management and Leadership (ILM), *Ambition and Gender at Work*, 2011.

Institute of Leadership & Management (ILM) and Management Today, *Index of Leadership Trust 2010*, ILM, September 2010, https://www.i-l-m.com/~/media/ILM%20Website/Documents/Information%20for%20centres/ILM_Index_Leadership_Trust_2010_Report%20pdf.ashx.

Jackson Hole Historical Society

Kabacoff, Robert, Ph.D., "The Glass Ceiling Revisited," Management Research Group, 2001.

Kaiser, R. B., "Leadership and the Fate of Organizations," *American Psychologist* 63 (2008): 96–110, 99.

Kalev, Alexandra, Erin Kelly, and Frank Dobbin, "Best Practices or Best Guesses? Assessing the Efficacy of Corporate Affirmative Action and Diversity Policies," *American Sociological Review* 71 (2006).

Kay, Katty, and Claire Shipman, Claire, "The Confidence Gap," *Atlantic*, May 2014, http://www.theatlantic.com/magazine/archive/2014/05/the-confidence-gap/359815/

Kay, Katty, and Claire Shipman, *The Confidence Code: The Science and Art of Self-Assurance—What Women Should Know* (New York: Harper Collins, 2014).

Kellogg School of Management, Northwestern University, "Leaders Do Matter—but When Does Their Gender Matter, Too?" Based on research of Susan E. Perkins, Katherine W. Phillips, and Nicholas Pearce, http://insight.kellogg.northwestern.edu/artile/leaders_do_matter_when_does_their_gender_matter_too.

Ketchum Inc., "2014 Ketchum Leadership Communication Monitor (KLCM)," May 2014, https://www.ketchum.com/leadership-communication-monitor-2014.

Killelea, Grace, *The Confidence Effect: Every Woman's Guide to the Attitude That Attracts Success*, American Management Association, 2016.

Kruse, Kevin, "What Is Leadership?" Forbes.com, April 9, 2013, http://www.forbes.com/sites/kevinkruse/2013/04/09/what-is-leadership/#1a5bddae713e.

Lai, Andrea. "Transformational-Transactional Leadership Theory," 2011 AHS Capstone Projects, Paper 17, http://digitalcommons.olin.edu/ahs_capstone_2011/17.

Larson, T. A., *History of Wyoming* (Lincoln: University of Nebraska Press, 1979).

LeanIn.org and McKinsey & Company, *Women in the Workplace*, 2015.

Ledbetter, Bernice, "5 Ways to Seize a New Opportunity with Confidence," *Huffington Post*, January 25, 2016.

Lieberman, Matthew D., *Social: Why Our Brains Are Wired to Connect*, (Oxford: Oxford University Press, 2013).

Lieberman, Matthew D., "Should Leaders Focus on Results, or on People?" *Harvard Business Review*, December 27, 2013, http://blogs.hbr.org/2013/12/should-leaders-focus-on-results-or-on-people.

Llopis, Glenn, "The Most Undervalued Leadership Traits of Women," Forbes.com, February 3, 2014, http://www.forbes.com/sites/glennllopis/2014/02/03/the-most-undervalued-leadership-traits-of-women/#7a6082c690c2.

Management Research Group, *Gender Differences and Leadership*, 2013.

Martin, Dan, "Do Women or Men Make the Best Leaders?" Business Zone, June 27, 2012, http://www.businesszone.co.uk/decide/scale/do-men-or-women-make-the-best-leaders.

McKinsey & Company, *Women Matter 3: Women Leaders, a Competitive Edge in and After the Crisis*, April 2010. http://www.mckinsey.com/global-themes/women-matter.

McKinsey Global Institute, *The Power of Parity: How Advancing Women's Equality Can Add $12 Trillion to Global Growth*, September 2015.

Millennials Intelligence Group Study, *Columbus Dispatch*, March 30, 2014.

Mollick, Ethan, "Why Are women Less Likely to be Entrepreneurs Than Men?" World Economic Forum Agenda, December 16, 2015.

Morse, Steven B., "Racial and Gender Differences in the Viability of Extremely Low Birth Weight Infants: A Population-Based Study," *Pediatrics* 117 (2006).

Netchaeva, Elaterina, Maryam Kouchaki, and Leah D. Sheppard, "A Man's (Precarious) Place: Men's Experienced Threat and Self-Assertive Reactions to Female Superiors," *Personal and Social Psychology Bulletin* 41, no. 9 (2015): 1247–1259.

Ning, Li, et al., "Achieving More with Less: Extra Milers' Behavioral Influences in Crews," *Journal of Applied Psychology* 100 (2015).

Perschel, Anne, and Jane Perdue, "Women and the Paradox of Power: 8 Keys for Transforming Business Culture," Women 2.0, January 2012, http://women2.com/2012/09/14/women-and-the-paradox-of-power-8-keys-for-transforming-business-culture/.

Pew Research Center, *Women and Leadership: Public Says Women Are Equally Qualified, but Barriers Persist*, January 2015, http://www.pewsocialtrends .org/2015/01/14/women-and-leadership.

Pfaff, Lawrence A. & Associates, "Perceptions of Women and Men Leaders Following 360-Degree Feedback Evaluations," *Performance Improvement Quarterly* 26 (2013), first published online April 17, 2013.

Prime, Jeanine L., and Nancy M. Carter, "Women 'Take Care,' Men 'Take Charge': Managers' Stereotypic Perceptions of Women and Men Leaders," *The Psychologist-Manager Journal* 12 (2009): 25–49.

Rashid Rehman, Rena, and Ajmal Wahee, "Transformational Leadership Style As a Predictor of Decision Making Styles: Moderating Role of Emotional Intelligence," *Pakistan Journal of Commerce and Social Sciences* 6 (2012): 257–268.

Reuben, Ernesto, Pedro Rey-Biel, Paola Sapienza, and Luigi Zingales, "The Emergence of Male Leadership in Competitive Environments," IZA, Discussion Paper No. 5300 November 2010, http://ftp.iza.org/dp5300.pdf.

Rivers, Caryl, and Rosalind C. Barnett, *The New Soft War on Women: How the Myth of Female Ascendance Is Hurting Women, Men—and Our Economy* (New York: Jeremy P. Tarcher/Penguin, 2013).

Ryan, Michelle K., S. Alexander Haslam, Mette D. Hersby, and Renata Bongiorno, "Think Crisis—Think Female. The Glass Cliff and Contextual Variation in the Think Manager—Think Male Stereotype," *Journal of Applied Psychology* 96 (2011): 470–484.

Sabic, Pavle, *How Times Have Changed? CEO Gender Gap Analysis of the S&P 500*; S&P Capital IQ, November 2015.

Sandberg, Sheryl, *Lean In: Women, Work, and the Will to Lead* (New York: Alfred A. Knopf, 2013).

Satterthwaite, Theodore et al., "Linked Sex Differences in Cognition and Functional Connectivity in Youth," *Cerebral Cortex* Oxford University Press, March 18, 2014, http://cercor.oxfordjournals.org/content/25/9/2383.abstract.

Sherwin, Bob, "Why Women Are More Effective Leaders Than Men," *Business Insider*, January 24, 2014, http://www.businessinsider.com/study-women-are-better-leaders-2014-1.

Scheer, Teva J., *Governor Lady: The Life and Times of Nellie Tayloe Ross*, Missouri Biography Series (Columbia, MO: University of Missouri Press, 2005).

Schutte, Shane, "Female CEOs: Business Turnaround Extraordinaires?," Real Business, October 28, 2013, http://realbusiness.co.uk/article/28252-female-ceos-business-turnaround-extraordinaires.

Snyder, Steven, "Why Resilience Is So Hard," *Harvard Business Review*, November 6, 2013, https://hbr.org/2013/11/why-is-resilience-so-hard/.

Tannen, Deborah, "The Power of Talk: Who Gets Heard and Why," *Harvard Business Review*, September/October 1995, https://hbr.org/1995/09/the-power-of-talk-who-gets-heard-and-why.

Tannen, Deborah, *Talking from 9 to 5* (New York: Morrow Publishing, 1994).

Tannen, Deborah. *You Just Don't Understand* (New York: Morrow Publishing, 1990).

Tate, Carson, "Are Confident People More Productive?," http://99u.com/articles/52305/are-confident-people-more-productive.

Tomova, L., et al., "Is Stress Affecting Our Ability to Tune into Others? Evidence for Gender Differences in the Effects of Stress on Self-Other Distinction," *Psychoneuroendrocrinology* 43 (2014): 95–104.

"Transformational Leadership a Route to Women's Promotion?" *The Leadership Quarterly* 22 (2011).

University of California, Irvine, "Intelligence in Men and Women Is a Gray and White Matter," Science Daily, January 22, 2005, https://www.sciencedaily.com/releases/2005/01/050121100142.htm.

Valero, Jesus N., Kyujin Jung, and Simon A. Andrew, "Does Transformational Leadership Build Resilient Public and Nonprofit Organizations?" *Disaster Prevention and Management* 24 (2015): 4–20.

Vanderkam, Laura, "The New Meaning Of Workplace Mentorship," *Fast Company*, January 10, 2016, http://www.fastcompany.com/3040938/the-new-meaning-of-workplace-mentorship.

Verma, Ragini, "Brain Connectivity Study Reveals Striking Differences Between Men and Women," Science Daily, December 2, 2013.

Vinkenburg, Claartje, Marloes L. van Engen, Alice H. Eagly, and Mary C. Johannesen-Schmidt, "An Exploration in Stereotypical Beliefs About Leadership Styles: Is Transformational Leadership a Route to Women's Promotion?" *The Leadership Quarterly* 22 (2011): 10–21.

Wang, G., "Transformational Leadership and Performance Across Criteria and Levels: A Meta-Analytics Review of 25 Years of Research," *Group and Organization Management* 36 (2011): 233–270.

Women in the Workplace, a study sponsored by McKenzie and Lean-In, September 2015. WomenintheWorkplace.com.

Zenger, Jack, and Joseph Folkman, "How Age and Gender Affect Self-Improvement," *Harvard Business Review*, January 5, 2016.

Zenger, Jack, and Joseph Folkman, "What Inspiring Leaders Do," *Harvard Business Review*, June 20, 2013.

Zenger, John H., and Joseph R. Folkman, *The Extraordinary Leader*: *Turning Good Managers into Great Leaders* (New York: McGraw Hill, 2009).

2011 HOW Report, LRN Corp, *Chief Learning Officer*, http://howmetrics.lrn.com.

Index

About the Author

Daina Middleton is currently head of leadership development at Larcen Consulting Group. With more than three decades of hands-on business experience as a leader and CEO, she spent the majority of her career in marketing and wrote *Marketing in the Participation Age: A Guide to Motivating People to Join, Share, Take Part, Connect, and Engage*, published in 2012.

Before her work in transformational leadership, Daina held a number of roles at Hewlett-Packard Company during her sixteen-year tenure there, where she pioneered digital marketing. She went on to be global CEO at Performics, the largest performance marketing company in the world, and ran global business marketing at Twitter. She currently serves as a director on the boards of Marin Software and Healthwise.

Daina is a frequent speaker, and her work has been published in *Forbes*, *Fast Company*, *The Huffington Post*, and *Adweek*, and she has appeared on CNBC.

She lives near Jackson Hole, Wyoming.

Daina's Work with Clients

Daina works with both men and women executives who understand the tremendous impact that leadership development can have on bringing their businesses to the next level. Additionally, she offers a unique program for women leaders designed to dramatically boost their leadership effectiveness and give them the tools to succeed in male-dominated industries.

Daina's Executive Development program has three components:

- Discovery and Self-Awareness
- Development and Action Plan
- Monthly Guiding Sessions

In addition to her Executive Development program, Daina offers condensed coaching at a select number of leadership events and workshops throughout the year.

To learn more about working with Daina on executive development, visit www.dainamiddleton.com.

Daina Middleton's Grace Meets Grit Keynote

Senior corporate executive, author, and leadership behavior expert Daina Middleton shares rare insight into the behaviors that drive leadership success in her newest keynote:

Grace Meets Grit: How to Bring Out
the Remarkable, Courageous Leader Within

In this keynote, Daina talks about lessons she learned in her own career and reveals how she achieved success at the highest levels in some of today's most male-dominated fields. She inspires and challenges women and men to view leadership through the Grace Meets Grit lens by providing insight into why and how men and women approach leadership behaviors differently, and by offering productive solutions that will help organizations drive behavioral change. Audiences leave empowered to recognize and embrace their unique strengths as leaders, equipped to leverage the "leadership superpowers" of others, and ready to make an immediate difference in the culture and effectiveness of their organizations.

To invite Daina to speak, or to learn more about this and other keynotes, visit her at www.dainamiddleton.com.

Get in touch!
I'd love to hear from you.

Visit me at dainamiddleton.com

Follow me on Twitter @DainaMiddleton

Join the conversation on Facebook at Daina Middleton